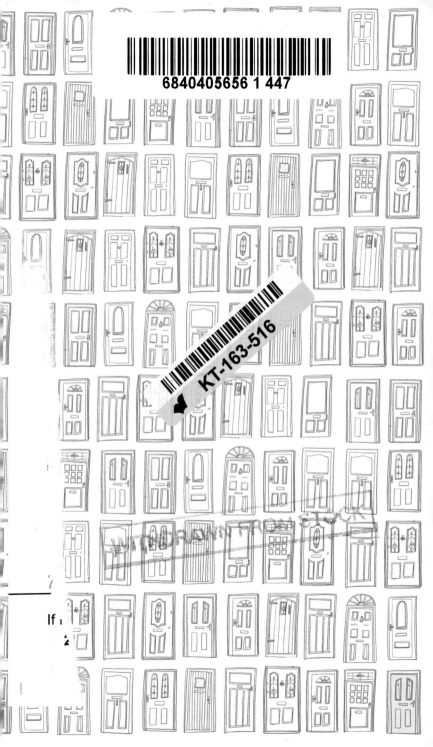

If
2

MY LIFE IN HOUSES

FICTION

Dames' Delight
Georgy Girl
The Bogeyman
The Travels of Maudie Tipstaff
The Park
Miss Owen-Owen is At Home
Fenella Phizackerley
Mr Bone's Retreat
The Seduction of Mrs Pendlebury
Mother Can You Hear Me?
The Bride of Lowther Fell
Marital Rites
Private Papers
Have the Men Had Enough?
Lady's Maid
The Battle for Christabel
Mother's Boys
Shadow Baby
The Memory Box
Diary of an Ordinary Woman
Is There Anything You Want?
Keeping the World Away
Over
Isa & May
The Unknown Bridesmaid

NON-FICTION

The Rash Adventurer: The Rise and Fall of Charles Edward Stuart
William Makepeace Thackeray: Memoirs of a Victorian Gentleman
Significant Sisters: The Grassroots of Active Feminism 1839–1939
Elizabeth Barrett Browning
Daphne du Maurier
Hidden Lives
Rich Desserts & Captain's Thin: A Family & Their Times 1831–1931
Precious Lives
Good Wives?: Mary, Fenny, Jenny and Me 1845–2001

POETRY

Selected Poems of Elizabeth Barrett Browning (Editor)

Margaret
FORSTER

My Life
in Houses

Chatto & Windus
LONDON

Published by Chatto & Windus 2014

4 6 8 10 9 7 5

Copyright © Margaret Forster 2014

Margaret Forster has asserted her right under the Copyright, Designs
and Patents Act 1988 to be identified as the author of this work

First published in Great Britain in 2014 by
Chatto & Windus
Random House, 20 Vauxhall Bridge Road,
London SW1V 2SA
www.randomhouse.co.uk

Addresses for companies within The Random House Group Limited can be
found at: www.randomhouse.co.uk/offices.htm

The Random House Group Limited Reg. No. 954009

A CIP catalogue record for this book
is available from the British Library

ISBN 9780701189105

Words from *Downhill all the Way* reproduced by kind permission of the
University of Sussex and Society of Authors as the Literary Representative of
the Estate of Leonard Woolf.

The Random House Group Limited supports the Forest Stewardship
Council® (FSC®), the leading international forest-certification organisation.
Our books carrying the FSC label are printed on FSC®-certified paper. FSC
is the only forest-certification scheme supported by the leading environmental
organisations, including Greenpeace. Our paper procurement policy can be
found at www.randomhouse.co.uk/environment

Typeset in Adobe Garamond by Palimpsest Book Production Limited,
Falkirk, Stirlingshire
Printed and bound in Great Britain by
CPI Group (UK) Ltd, Croydon, CR0 4YY

Facts about the houses in which one lives during the whole journey from the womb to the grave are not unimportant. The house – in which I include its material and spiritual environment – has an immense influence on its inhabitants . . . what has the deepest and most permanent effect upon oneself and one's way of living is the house in which one lives. The house determines the day-to-day, minute-to-minute quality, colour, atmosphere, pace of one's life; it is the framework of what one does, of what one can do, of one's relations with people . . . looking back on my life, I tend to see it divided into sections which are determined by the houses in which I have lived, not by school, university, work, marriage, death, division, or war.

Leonard Woolf, *Downhill All the Way: An Autobiography*

Contents

ORTON ROAD

Carlisle

I was born on 25th May 1938, in the front bedroom of a house in Orton Road, a house on the outer edge of Raffles, a council estate.

I was a lucky girl. Carlisle City Council was quite flushed with pride over this estate, consisting as it did of two thousand houses. It had responded with enthusiasm to the King's speech of April 1919, in which he had said the only adequate solution to so many of the population living in inadequate housing was to build more houses specifically for the poor. There were lots of 'the poor' in Carlisle, many of them crammed into slum dwellings in Caldewgate, where most of the factories were situated. In 1920, a report on the Sanitary Condition of the City of Carlisle had condemned the majority of dwellings in Caldewgate as 'unfit for habitation' yet they were all heavily inhabited. The report spoke of 'a bad arrangement of lanes and courts', pointing out how few houses had an internal water supply, and that none had their own lavatory. The yards in 'common' use meant infectious diseases spread rapidly. It was this dire situation that the new council estate, to the north-west of Caldewgate, was built to redress: to get these 'poor' out into the green fields of Raffles.

My parents, though, couldn't be categorised as belonging to 'the poor', but the council was enlightened enough to realise that for the future health of the new estate it might be a good idea to have a few young married couples, just starting off, mixed in with families removed from the slums. My father, a fitter working in Hudson Scott's factory, at least qualified as a manual worker (ninety-one per cent of those allocated houses were manual workers). My mother, who up to marrying in 1931 was a secretary in the Health Department, was strictly speaking a class above him, but, as all women did, she had to give up her job once they married. Both of them were born in Carlisle, and both lived in houses owned by their parents, small terraced houses in working-class areas but nevertheless owned, not rented. They could well have had to start off married life living with one or other of their parents so they were pleased to be able to rent a new house of their very own, at six shillings a week, just under a quarter of my father's weekly wage.

They had both been familiar with the fields of Raffles before the estate was built. The ninety-eight acres purchased by the council stretched either side of the road leading west to Wigton. Not much had ever grown there, except poor-quality grass, because the soil was thick with clay and drainage was difficult. The new estate wasn't spoiling a beautiful area of countryside. In any case, the idea was that Raffles should be a housing estate of the garden city variety with great care to be given to its layout. There were to be lots of green spaces left, and only twelve houses built on any one acre, with a pleasing mixture of terraces and semi-detached dwellings. There was to be a church, shops and a park. It would be a model of its kind.

The estate had just been completed when my parents moved into Orton Road in 1931. The house was on a corner, facing into Orton Road which skirted the western side of the estate. It was semi-detached, with a garden on three sides. Inside, there was a living room, a tiny back kitchen, two bedrooms and a bathroom where there was indeed a bath but no sink or lavatory. The lavatory was part of the fabric of the house but could only be reached by going out of the backdoor and into the adjoining outhouse. There had been huge arguments about this at council meetings, mainly over the expense of putting lavatories in bathrooms. Clearly that was ruled out. But the less-expensive possibility of simply knocking through into the outside lavatory from the kitchen was not gone into. Good heavens, these people should be grateful to have their own lavatory even if they often had to get soaked going out to it. And they were.

My parents were ideal tenants. They looked after their rented house perfectly. This maintenance was not easy. The house was heated by an open fire set in the black iron range which filled one wall of the living room. The black leading of this range was an unpleasant job, one that hadn't changed from Victorian times, and the laying and cleaning out of the coal fire was a wearying task. Because of this coal fire, there was always a lot of dust so keeping things clean was a constant challenge. Luckily, perhaps, there was not much furniture to keep clean: a settee, an armchair, a table, four wooden chairs and a sideboard, most bought in auctions. Quite enough, though, to make the fourteen by twelve foot room look crowded. In the back kitchen there was a gas cooker and a sink, with a wooden board to the left of the sink which served as a worktop. Upstairs, in the room where I was to be born, there was a double bed, a wardrobe, a dressing table and a chest of drawers. Later, when there were three children, an alcove was turned into a Scottish-style bed-in-the-wall, or in other words a mattress was put on top of a board laid across the alcove, with a curtain rigged up in front of it to give an illusion of privacy. There was another small bedroom at the back, in which, for a while, my maternal grandmother stayed, until she died in 1936.

By the time I was born, things were still going well for Raffles, Carlisle's pride and joy. The new park, in particular, was a showpiece. Opened in 1934, it had a miniature golf course and a paddling pool as well as lots of open spaces for children to play. The new church was like a glistening white palace, set almost in the centre of the estate, and well attended. Strangely, there was no school. Children either had to go to Ashley Street, on the edge of Caldewgate, or Newtown, outside the estate at the other end. The estate still looked sparklingly clean, the roads well swept, the gardens established and, mostly, thriving and well looked after.

So there I was, born in a house in Orton Road, eager to see if the house itself would indeed determine the 'quality, colour, atmosphere and pace' of my life.

It certainly did.

I lived in Orton Road for fourteen years. It was, by any standards, a good house for any child to live in. The fire always burned brightly, there was always food on the table, and that table was covered with a pristine tablecloth for every meal. The sideboard was never without a vase of flowers, picked from our own garden, and the brass ornaments sitting on it were regularly polished. Everything was always tidy, clean and neat. Dishes were never left unwashed, floors never went unswept. Housework was hard, with no labour-saving devices whatsoever, but it was done with back-breaking efficiency. It was a good house to come home to, but by the time I was seven I'd found ways of being in it as little as possible. The truth was I preferred other houses. The ones which lay on the other side of Orton Road.

Orton Road was a demarcation line. On one side, our side, was the Raffles council estate; on the other were the privately owned houses. Directly opposite our house was the opening to Inglewood Crescent, lined either side with houses that had proper bathrooms, dining rooms as well as sitting rooms, kitchens with (for the 1940s) all mod cons, and upstairs three bedrooms. This crescent seemed to me to epitomise gracious living. Even the concrete road surface, which had stayed almost white, seemed superior to the tarmac roads of our estate. At the top of this crescent were open fields, giving a country feel. The children living in these houses went, on the whole, to the same primary schools as we on the Raffles estate did, so I had friends among them. As soon as I got home from Ashley Street School, I'd be dashing over to some house or other in Inglewood Crescent where I'd collect my friends and we'd go off to play in the disused tennis court behind the houses at the top of the crescent. We used an old hut there as a stage and put on 'shows'. Only when it rained heavily, or began to grow dark, did we go home. I'd usually manage to wriggle my way into one of the crescent houses for a short while before crossing Orton Road to my own house, wishing passionately that we lived in Inglewood Crescent.

The attraction was the space. In our house, we five – my parents, me, an older brother and a younger sister – were all crammed into one living room where we ate and sat, with the wireless nearly always on. In the Inglewood Crescent houses people were not all obliged to be together. There were electric fires in the different rooms, even some of the bedrooms, so family togetherness was not obligatory. I didn't see my longing for space as any rejection of my own family, just as a natural desire to have the chance not to be forced to be with others all the time. There was one friend, an only child, whose house I particularly liked to be in and luckily her parents liked having me there. I was considered a suitable companion, even though I might have been thought from the wrong side of Orton Road (Raffles by then having begun to be thought 'rough'). But then this friend's father was made Station Master of Silloth Station and they moved. My friend missed me, and soon I was invited to spend the weekend with her in Station House, Silloth.

My father, who had a great reverence for all things to do with trains and stations, and whose favourite outing was to the little seaside town of Silloth, was very impressed by my good fortune in getting such an invitation. 'Station House' conjured up all sorts of visions for me, though in fact I should have known perfectly well what it looked like because I'd been going to Silloth by train, together with half the population of Carlisle, all my life. It was just that I'd never really looked at the house. I knew it was big, and right opposite the entrance to the station, but there was always such a rush, straight from train to sea, that I'd never taken in what kind of house it was except that it stood on its own. The reality was a little forbidding. Station House was a large, red-brick house, set back slightly from the road. There was a big window to the left of the front door, which had a pointed roof at the top. To the right was a smaller window. There were no flowers growing in the garden, just some dark green shrubs, sprawling and overgrown. The front door was painted black, and had a lion's head as a knocker. These ground-floor windows either side had net curtains over them which to me made it look as though the house had its eyes closed. Inside, it seemed rather dark in the hallway, the only light coming from a landing window. The only two rooms downstairs actually in use were the kitchen, at the back, and the sitting room leading off it. Both seemed vast, and were sparsely furnished. The family – just my friend and her parents – had moved from a modern semi-detached in Carlisle to this large house and their furniture seemed lost in it.

I'd never imagined that a house could dominate the people in it, but that was what this house did. Every footstep taken echoed, and though my friend and I ran around and made plenty of noise, the moment we sat down the intense silence of the rooms closed in. Their dog, an Alsatian, which, in the house in Carlisle, had seemed too big and energetic for it, here seemed cowed. I did not feel comfortable there even though, theoretically, this was the kind of house I'd wanted to live in. Luckily, we were out most of the time, playing on Silloth Green. My friend had started going to Allonby, a seaside village a couple of miles down the coast, to ride, and that weekend I was asked if I would like to ride too. I said yes at once. Nobody asked if I *could* ride, though surely my friend's parents must have known it was unlikely. Anyway, I firmly believed I could. Had I not ridden donkeys on Silloth Green on day trips from Carlisle, many a time? Of course I had – nothing to it. And in all the stories I read all the children rode, galloping away, just as I was confident I would be able to do. I could see myself, in a pair of borrowed jodhpurs, wearing one of those special caps, astride a chestnut mare, racing along Allonby sands . . .

At least the riding instructor quickly realised I'd never even sat on a horse in my life. I couldn't get in the saddle without considerable assistance, and when I got there I couldn't sit upright without enormous effort. My horse, doubtless the most docile in the stable, was put on a leading rein, and we only trotted while the others galloped. For a while I was nevertheless in love with my own image of myself, a girl who could ride and lived in a *big house* by the sea, so exciting. At the end of the lesson, I could hardly get off the horse and when I slithered off I could barely walk. For the rest of my three-day stay at Station House I was in agony, though by the time I got home I was already boasting about my ride, how wonderful it had been.

I was invited again to Station House, but I never went. Ever after, I averted my eyes when I came out of Silloth station.

Another big house influenced me soon after, but this house was a school. At eleven, I passed the eleven plus and went to the Carlisle & County High School for Girls in Lismore Place. The building overawed me. Built in 1909, at a cost of £18,000, it was in the style of an Edwardian mansion, with a lawn in front, used as tennis courts in the summer, and enough land around it to provide ample playing fields. Walking into this building every day thrilled me, especially going into the assembly hall with its stage, and scholarship boards on the walls, and the balcony running along one side. I would like to have lived there, and as it was hung about at the end of each school day, reluctant to leave. Unlike Station House, there didn't seem to me to be anything intimidating or depressing about this much larger 'house'. It seemed full of light, and I failed to notice that by then (1949) the fabric was showing signs of deterioration. I saw only the space. I marvelled at the vastness of the place. My fantasy was that it would become a boarding school (the fees paid by the Council, of course). Going home to Orton Road was a terrible let-down.

But going to-and-from school also taught me a lot about other houses. There were so many different kinds between Orton Road and Lismore Place. I was already thoroughly familiar with semi-detached houses, but Chiswick Street, or Warwick Road, had quite different buildings. These were three-storey Victorian terraced houses, with doors and windows quite unlike those belonging to the houses on the Raffles estate. The doors in particular impressed me. They looked as though they could keep an army out, they were so solid. Looking at the windows, counting them, I reckoned some of these houses had eight rooms in them, and I wondered what they were all used for. The streets they stood in were quite broad and I liked walking down them. The contrast not just with where I'd started from but with the medieval lanes I'd cut through (once I'd got off the Ribble bus at the Town Hall, to get to them), was marked. There were not many people still living in those lanes by then, but I'd been in some of the tiny, crammed-together houses there and knew how dark and dismal they were. There was a whole history lesson just in contrasting all the various houses, though I had no knowledge then of what it was.

But I knew that any kind of house was preferable to the alternative, a flat or a bed-sitting room. My aunt Jean, my mother's sister, lived in what was really a flat, though it had the appearance of a house. Number 366 Bellshill Road in Motherwell had a proper front door so that it looked as if it led to a house, but once inside it was revealed as a flat. There were just two rooms and a tiny kitchen area on a landing at the top of a flight of steps which led down to lower ground level, passing a flat below on the way. She and her husband and two sons lived here in this big block, known as The Buildings. Out at the back was a line of washhouses, and further along an old slag heap called 'the bing' where children played. There was a strong communal atmosphere among the women using the washhouses – they all knew each other, and were in and out of each other's 'houses' all the time. Coming home to Orton Road after staying with Aunt Jean I suddenly appreciated what we had there. Slowly, it was beginning to dawn on me that it was all a matter of comparisons. I might yearn for the space and privacy a big house gave you but compared to living in 'The Buildings' I already had it.

Just to confuse things, there was another sort of flat within my experience. My mother's other sister, Nan, lived with her husband and son in a flat above an opticians' in Nottingham. If we weren't spending our holidays in Motherwell, we spent them in Nottingham in an entirely different flat. This one was large, with three bedrooms, and a spacious living room, kitchen and bathroom. It was comfortably furnished, with pale-coloured fitted carpets throughout, and silk curtains at the windows. There was no garden or outside space but otherwise it seemed to me an attractive place to live. I could live in such a place, I thought, having previously decided I would never want to live in a flat. But of course in Aunt Nan's flat there was no one living above and no one living below (because below was the shop). So it felt quite separate, suffering none of the common disadvantages of flat-dwelling. Still, no garden was a minus, and I went home from this flat grudgingly grateful to live in a house that had one.

I was still, at eleven years old, playing at my version of houses the way other girls played at skipping. It obsessed me. The game consisted of fixing upon an existing house in Carlisle's Norfolk Road, down which we walked to visit our grandparents. In this road, which had no access to traffic at one end, making it very quiet, there were double-fronted Victorian or Edwardian villas, some approached by circular drives, and with imposing iron gates at the entrance, often with stone pillars either side. One or two, at the end of the 1940s, had already been converted into old people's homes but most were still privately owned and lived in by solicitors and managing directors of local firms. This was not in Carlisle's posh area (that was

Stanwix) but this one road, despite being a little too near the Raffles estate, was a desirable road to live in. In my imagination, in this game I played, I already lived in it, though I changed 'my' house regularly. I selected a house and moved out the people living in it. Where to? I had no idea – they were just evicted, it was their problem where they were to go. I took over the minute they had gone, just me, not with my family. I chose a bedroom at the back of whichever house it was, hoping that it looked out onto a garden full of apple trees. (I couldn't see how big the gardens of these houses were, but I was sure they must have lawns and trees.) I wouldn't have curtains at the window, just a blind, the sort I'd seen pictures of in magazines. The walls would be plain white, and the carpet pale green. There would be no dark furniture in this room, everything would be light wood. I hesitated over my bed: brass headboard, or wickerwork? Then I moved into the rest of the house, cautiously investigating room after room, and changing the decor in seconds. There would definitely be a library, though I wasn't sure how to fit in shelves, whether they should go right round the walls or, as in the Tullie House public library, be free-standing. Oh, problems, problems, all of them delightful.

I played this game but I hardly played at all with the doll's house I had. It was no good to me, with my grandiose ideas. My father's brother, Bob, had made it for me when I was seven. It turned out to be deeply disappointing, consisting as it did of a roof over four square rooms, two above, an identical two below, and all of them open at the front. There was no hinged door to close the house so that it would look like a real house. That, I suppose, was beyond Bob's capabilities. After a few half-hearted attempts to paint the rooms and stick bits of plastic on the floors, and scraps of wool to act as carpets, I lost interest. The few bits of doll's furniture I was given looked ridiculous in this open house, and moving them about was no fun at all. I expect I was thought unappreciative, but luckily for me it soon didn't matter because my father had a row with Bob and they didn't speak to each other for the next forty years. Even then, it wasn't a proper conversation. Bob came to my mother's funeral and seeing him standing respectfully outside the church, my father bellowed through the opened car window: 'Bob, you can come to the tea if you want.' Bob shook his head. That was that. The non-speaking continued to the death. After their row, though, the doll's house became tainted, and I was allowed to give it away. Far better to play houses in my head.

But there was another house, apart from those in Norfolk Road, which fascinated me, and which I thought I could see myself one day living in, if some magic occurred. Morton Manor was just across the Wigton Road, which marked the far edge of the Raffles estate. It couldn't actually be seen because it had a long, high wall separating the grounds it stood in from the road, but once a year Sir Robert and Lady Chance held a garden fete there and we were allowed in, making our way through the big gates and along the driveway which on either side was dense with shrubs and trees. There had been a house on that site since the seventeenth century but the manor as it was that day (or parts of it) had been there since 1807, when the Forster family bought and added to it. The Forster family? How lucky that I didn't know this in the 1940s, when I would immediately have spun a fantasy about myself really belonging to *this* branch of the Border family famously mentioned in Walter Scott's 'Young Lochinvar' and not my own – I'd have cast myself as the long-lost great-granddaughter, the rightful heir. As it was, John Forster sold the manor in 1837, and eventually it came to belong to Robert Chance.

Coming upon the house was a surprise – it was hidden for so long from visitors winding their way along the drive. The gardens were natural-looking but in fact cleverly designed by a celebrated nineteenth-century gardener, William Sawrey Gilpin. I didn't know anything about garden design and had never heard of Gilpin, but I could see that the Morton Manor gardens were artistic. So was the manor itself. It was a long, low building, just two storeys high, with floor-to-ceiling windows on the ground floor and quite a modest entrance to the house through a curved porch. The whole of this front wall was covered with ivy (though maybe it was Virginia creeper – I never saw it in the autumn). I thought this made it romantic, but my father looked at it and condemned it at once on two grounds: ivy weakened the wall, and it encouraged insects which would get into the rooms. I wondered if I should pass this worrying information on to Sir Robert and Lady Chance, who that day sometimes came among us, but decided not to. We were not, of course, allowed into the house, but I lurked near the generous windows and tried to peer in, ever so casually. I couldn't see much, just what looked like heavy dark furniture and some large, dark pictures on the walls.

Coming home from Morton Manor, I instantly pictured our council house covered with ivy. It looked much better. But nothing could be done about how the house looked, ivy or no ivy. It looked like a child's drawing, and a child who had no talent for drawing. It was crude in shape, even I could see that without knowing anything about architecture. There were no distinguishing features – well, of course there weren't, the council's money wouldn't run to anything fancy. The front door, like all the other houses on the estate, was painted a dismal shade of green, not fern green, not forest green, but a withered-cabbage green. I looked at it more and more critically once I'd grown accustomed to other styles of houses. I noticed how the top half of the walls, which were rendered, had turned a dirty grey, and I wished they could be whitewashed. That would help. So would reorganising the shape of the garden. Most of it was to the side, which made it very public. If it had been at the back, there would have been some privacy . . . on and on I went, fixing my general discontent on the poor house.

But at least I recognised that, badly arranged

though it was, our garden was a showpiece, though not of the Morton Manor variety. Gilpin, I imagine, wouldn't have approved of cabbages and rhubarb growing together with roses, but he would surely have admired my father's hedges. These were superbly maintained, though they needed constant trimming. Privet grows rapidly and densely, but my father, who liked it four-feet high and two-feet wide, tamed it, and all with hand-shears. However, every Friday night this front hedge took a cruel bashing, to my father's fury. A few hundred yards to the left of our house, where Orton Road met Wigton Road, there had once been a tollgate, when Raffles consisted of open fields. An inn had stood there since the early nineteenth century, named The Horse & Farrier (probably because the publican was also the blacksmith). A new pub, still called The Horse & Farrier, was built in the same place in the late 1920s, all ready to serve the thirsty inhabitants of the about-to-be-built council estate. There was no other pub on the estate so the popularity of The Horse & Farrier was assured. Our house was on the main route to it. When the publican turned the inebriated out at closing time, a great mass of roaring, fighting men (and a few women) would surge along Orton Road, making the first stop at our hedge, some men clinging on to it for support, some being sick into its glossy leaves, and some propelled into it by a fist. I'd lie with my younger sister Pauline in the bed-in-the-wall, my heart thudding, though I knew I was in no danger whatsoever, and listen to my father yelling out of the window that he was going to call the police (this would've been difficult as we had no telephone). Sometimes, his fury would grow so great he'd go and fill a bucket with water and throw it over the drunks. Not a wise move, though temporarily effective.

The Horse & Farrier was an imposing building, unlike any of the other pubs I'd passed in nearby Caldewgate. It would've been easy to mistake it for a rather grand house, situated as it was on a corner, all by itself, and with a bowling green behind it which could've been taken for a beautifully maintained lawn of best Solway Firth turf. The rendered walls were whitewashed annually and, like St Barnabas Church, deep in the heart of our estate, there was a certain glitter about the place. But I was afraid of it. My father patronised it himself, once a week, though he never came home drunk. I hated our house being near it. I never, when describing where I lived, said 'near The Horse & Farrier'. Instead, I'd say 'near Morton Park', or 'near Inglewood Crescent', snob-bery already in place.

It also featured large in the nightmares I regularly had. I'd never, of course, been inside this pub but in these nightmares I'd be in it with hordes of people all around me shouting and singing and cursing, all of them holding glasses of foaming beer in their hands, some of which slopped over and dripped on my head and ran down into my mouth. I was always on my knees, trying to crawl between the booted feet, and getting kicked as I struggled towards a door I could see ahead. This door was always open, with the light streaming into the dark room, and eventually I'd reach it and crawl through and stand up to walk away – at which point, I'd wake up, having fallen down the stairs. Fortunately, there were only twelve quite shallow stairs in our house, with a bend at the top which I'd obviously negotiated successfully in my sleep before falling. I was never really hurt. I'd be picked up, and taken to sit on my mother's knee and attempts would be made to try to find out what all this falling down the stairs had been about. I don't think I was ever able to describe the nightmare except to say I was in The Horse & Farrier, which completely mystified my mother.

Once the nightmare faded, and I was put back to bed, our house seemed an attractively safe place, even cosy, and I'd be relieved and glad to be tucked up in the bed-in-the-wall. But what I really liked, the time when the house took on another character entirely and I was quite happy living in it, was when it was empty except for me. This was rare. Usually, every evening, we were all in the living room with the wireless on, but sometimes on Friday evenings everyone would be out. Gordon, who was a keen Boy Scout, would be out at a Scouts meeting, or often away a whole weekend at a Scout camp; my mother sometimes would take Pauline to visit a relative. My father would come home from work, strip off his blue overalls, get washed and spruced up, then go for his end-of-the-week treat to The Horse & Farrier. They didn't all leave, or return, at the same time but there was usually at least an hour when the house was empty except for me. By the time I was twelve, it was considered allowable for me to be on my own, with strict instructions, in the winter, to keep an eye on the fire. It had to be regularly stoked up, and I hadn't to get so lost in a book that I failed to add coal at the appropriate time. When the house was empty, reading took on a different quality. It was not a

battle against noise and interruptions, and general resentment at what was considered an anti-social activity, but
instead an easy pleasure, with no effort needed to block
out everything happening in the room. I fantasised that
the house approved of my reading, that it enjoyed the
little library it had become. What I was actually reading
was mostly still children's stuff, Arthur Ransome and such
like, though I'd read *Jane Eyre* and had attempted Virginia
Woolf (*Orlando*, of which I made nothing whatsoever). It
was always annoying when the rest of the family began
arriving home and the house once more became more like
a busy meeting place than a library.

I'd disappear then upstairs, to the freezing-cold
bedroom, but at least by then, in 1950 and aged twelve
and nine respectively, my sister and I had graduated from
the bed-in-the-wall to the back bedroom because our
brother had gone off to do his National Service. We still
had to share a bed, but it was a proper and much more
comfortable bed, and it was a whole room to ourselves.
There was no space to fit in a desk or table but I sat at
the washstand to do my homework. This was a pretty
piece of furniture which had come from my maternal
grandmother's house. It was made of pine, and on it stood

a china jug and bowl. The jug was meant to be filled with hot water from the sink in the kitchen then carried up and poured into the bowl, to be used to wash. In fact, we all washed at the kitchen sink and only visitors (always family) got the washstand treatment. But with this jug and bowl moved to one side, a chair could be put in front of the washstand and I could just about sit at it to do my homework, though it meant jamming my knees under it or twisting them to one side.

Soon after we took occupation of this room, the art teacher at my school set as our homework 'The view from my bedroom window'. If I'd still been in my parents' bedroom in the bed-in-the-wall, whatever could I have painted? As it was, I had a proper window to look out of. I looked. It was a dreary view: the coal bunker, the rope washing line held up by two massive wooden props, and the backs of the nearest other council houses. All the flowers my father grew were at the side and the front of the house, the wonderfully varied lupins, and dahlias, and snapdragons which would have given me a whole paintbox of colours to play with. If I painted the real view, all I'd need was grey, black and brown. There was one tiny yellowish flower that grew in a damp little dip in the tarmac near the coal bunker, but I could hardly make anything of that. Slowly, I began to paint what I would have liked to have been seeing. A smooth, oval lawn came first, with an apple tree at the far end. I was about to cover it with blossom when I remembered it was November. In the centre of the brilliantly green lawn I put a fountain, but then couldn't paint the water so quickly altered it to a bird bath. No need to paint more than a black smudge to indicate a possible bird. I added a swing to a branch of the apple tree but knew I wasn't accomplished enough to attempt a figure sitting on it. Masses of gaudy flowers went in, all around the lawn, and in a moment of inspiration I managed quite a successful cat stalking across it (we had no pets). It was a startlingly colourful picture and I was pleased with it. No one at the High School had been to my house, least of all the teacher, and no one could possibly know this view was entirely untruthful, so I couldn't be found out. I handed in my homework with some pride, only to learn a shaming lesson. The best picture was painted by another girl whose view from her window was far more depressing and dreary than mine. She obviously lived in a house with no garden, only a yard, a yard full of dust and bins, one of them overflowing.

There was a rusty old bicycle lying on the ground, one wheel missing, and the colours she'd used were grey, a deeper grey, a pale grey, dark brown and black. She had rendered the scene truthfully and made a picture that was full of atmosphere and interest, however dismal. My own fantasy view had been ridiculous.

But then fantasising, or daydreaming, was how I lived my life. All the time. The house I lived in kept trying to pin me down to reality and I kept resisting and floating away. I would *not* be living here. I wouldn't let Orton Road be all there was in life. I would not have people looking at me and thinking 'ah, yes, Orton Road' reflected there. The idea of my place of dwelling somehow leaving an imprint on my character would have been anathema to me. I knew, already, that it was not possible to tell what kind of house someone lived in just from looking at them. There were girls at my school from all kinds of houses and until I'd visited their homes I hadn't been able to tell. Posh accents were rare in Carlisle in the 1950s, so voices didn't indicate where a girl probably lived. The state of a uniform wasn't an indication either – there was no such thing as a smart gymslip, and though some might be scruffier than others that could often be deliberate. No, it was no good guessing. Only the address gave anything away.

All my particular friends lived in privately owned houses of varying degrees of affluence. Not one was from Raffles, or any other council estate, not that I knew this before they became my friends. It was just chance. I loved going to their respective houses; I was still fascinated by the whole business of houses. They all had not only beds of their own but whole rooms, which they could retreat to and where they could do whatever they wanted. These rooms were often small but they'd been able to choose what colour the walls were painted and what to put on them. I'd never heard of Virginia Woolf's *A Room of One's Own*, but in these friends' rooms I understood how enviable it was to have such a room. You could go into it and shut the door and be private. What did privacy for a twelve-year-old bring? Remarkably little, only the pleasure of withdrawing from adult eyes and sibling annoyances. We lolled on the bed or the floor and talked, and that was about it. Eventually, we'd re-emerge, looking as if something important had been achieved. We'd spill into other rooms, carrying on the endless stream of inconsequential chatter. There were things in these rooms which

I'd never seen before, cocktail cabinets and gramophones, and in the hall there was always a telephone. In the kitchen, there was always a refrigerator which friends would fling open, offering me cold orange squash. I could never quite get used to all this largesse, never move about these houses comfortably, always feeling I should be on tiptoe, taking care not to spoil anything.

I never invited any of my High School chums to Orton Road. I didn't explain why. They didn't ask, or make hints that a return of hospitality would be welcome. It wasn't so much that where I lived embarrassed me – though, shockingly, it did – but that I couldn't think what we would do once we got home. Where could I take them? I didn't have a room of my own, and in any case most of the year the back bedroom was a sub-zero temperature. All excuses, of course, but they felt real to me. There was no reason whatsoever why I couldn't have brought friends home and stayed in the living room. My mother would've been friendly and polite, she'd have offered her excellent just-baked scones or cake, and my sister, who was quite shy, would have sat quietly, and at that time of day my brother and father would've been at work. So, I was being stupid as well as snobbish. I even recognised my attitude as snobbish, and knew it was a disgraceful thing, but I blamed the *house* for it, not myself.

I was not, though, only imagining that by 1950 the Raffles estate had begun to have an unfortunate reputation. The 'garden city' ideal had been lost. In the twenty years since it had been built, with such high ideals, and with such care, the estate had visibly changed. There were still houses like our own which were immaculately maintained, but there were also far more which looked neglected. There was, as yet, no drug culture, and no gangs, but certain roads had a run-down appearance and the shops had never really flourished. There was a good deal of alcoholism which led to fights in some streets, including ours, and police cars regularly appeared on Friday and Saturday nights. The reputation Raffles was earning was partly unjust but it stuck. All the people who lived there were lumped together: it was the people, it was said, the sort of people who lived there, the problem families, the rough types who didn't care about anything. We were not a problem family and we were not rough, but we were from Raffles, enough said, so far as some people were concerned.

There were other council estates in Carlisle,

33

however, which had different reputations. Longsowerby was reckoned the best of them. It had been the first one built, in 1922, and there had been no hesitation in providing the houses with indoor lavatories and (for some of them) even parlours. It was a showcase council estate and it had not slipped, by the 1950s, in the pecking order. There were only six-hundred houses and from the beginning tenants who could well have afforded to rent private accommodation had moved in and set the tone. This was where my mother wanted to move to, but moving at all when you were a Raffles tenant was a fraught business. The need, though, by 1952 was pressing. My brother was due home after completing his National Service, and once he reclaimed the back bedroom my sister and I (by then eleven and fourteen) would have to move back into the bed-in-the-wall in my parents' bedroom, or else my brother would have to give up his room and sleep in the living room. Neither solution was exactly attractive.

So, my mother started writing letters to the housing department of the council and at the same time looking for swaps in the local newspaper. She wrote a good letter, listing the reasons why she felt we had a case to be rehoused, preferably on the Longsowerby estate. I thought one of her reasons was a mistake. She said her father-in-law, recently widowed, who lived in a terrace house at the foot of the Longsowerby estate, was becoming frail and needed looking after. This would be easier if we were near at hand, on the Longsowerby estate. I thought the council might say, well, if you want to look after him and he lives in his own private house, why don't you move in with him? Problem solved. The council didn't bother suggesting this, which was just as well. My mother would've been appalled at the thought, hating as she did my grandfather's dark, narrow house which had no garden, only a small yard opening onto a back lane. I never really understood her objections. I looked at my grandfather's house and saw only the number of rooms – three bedrooms, a parlour – and the address: not on a council estate. I didn't want to live with him – he was a surly, grumpy man – but my idea was to put him in our Orton Road house. I was told not to be ridiculous. My mother was told by the council that all it could suggest was that she should put a request for a swap in the *Cumberland News*.

This she did. Every Friday, she also scrutinised the 'exchanges wanted' column. There were lots of these but while three-bedroom houses on all the estates in Carlisle were heavily in demand nobody seemed to want two-bedroom houses with no indoor lavatory. Especially not in Raffles. Then, suddenly, the possibility of an exchange came up. The tension in our house was terrific. 'Count on nothing,' my mother instructed us, but she was obviously hopeful herself. It seemed a man who had only one leg wanted to move to be near his daughter who lived in Raffles. He lived in Richardson Street, Longsowerby, exactly where my mother wanted to be. It appeared to be crucial that we had a bath in our bathroom though not a sink or lavatory. All the time the proposed exchange was being discussed and fretted over, the man's one leg seemed somehow of huge significance, though what on earth it had to do with it I cannot now imagine. He'd apparently been in his Longsowerby house, originally with two legs, since 1928, and had lost a leg in the Second World War. His house had not only three bedrooms but a parlour, and a parlour *with a bay window*.

The rent, if the exchange went through, would be more, which was a cause of great concern. Could the extra rent be managed? Just about, if my father did even more overtime. There was a brief moment when my mother, who had worked in Carlisle's Health Department as an assistant to the medical officer, and had once gone back for three months to fill in for someone who was ill, suggested that she could go back to work, but my father vetoed this immediately. He wasn't having that. I think my mother would have liked to return to her job, or one like it, but she didn't put up a fight.

Finally the exchange was agreed, and a date fixed, and my mother set to making sure that we would be leaving Orton Road in sparkling condition. The cleaning that went on those last two weeks was ferocious even though the house, it seemed to me, was already spotless. She made my father distemper the living room again, worried that when the battered old settee was removed there would be a mark on the wall. I even helped by scrubbing, on hands and knees, the linoleum in our bedroom.

There wasn't much to pack up, but enough to fill the van which my brother borrowed. My mother didn't really want to take our existing furniture ('poor stuff' she called it) but as there was no chance of buying new furniture she had to accept everything we had would be going with us. I don't know how she really felt about leaving a house she'd lived in for twenty-one years, ever since she'd been married. I was jubilant, but then I saw only the huge advantages and wasn't the slightest affected by nostalgia for the place. But my mother, inevitably, had memories that made this humble house mean something to her that transcended its bricks and mortar. Her own mother had died here; I'd been born here. And she had good friends, as I had, across the road in Inglewood Crescent. She would still see them, but it would mean at arranged times, no more slipping in and out of each other's houses.

As for my father, he was worried about the extra rent, and the expense of moving (though I couldn't see what that would be) and furthermore there was one thing about the one-legged man's house to which we were moving that he did not like at all: it was opposite the cemetery.

I came across a remark in *Howards End*, many years after I left the house where I was born, which struck me as mad. A character in this novel says: 'Can what they call civilisation be right, if people mayn't die in the room where they were born?' The idea of dying in that house in Orton Road, of wanting to die in the room where I was born, filled me with dismay.

But I once, in the 1980s, went back there to do a feature for a colour magazine, one in a series called 'The House Where I Grew Up'. It wasn't as though I hadn't been past the house many times since I left it – it was part of going back to Carlisle, which we did regularly, to do the nostalgia tour, driving round places that had some familial significance – so there was no real surprise to find the appearance of Orton Road quite different from how it had looked in 1952 when we left it. My father's beautifully tended garden had vanished. No neat and tidy lawns, no flower beds full of lupins and dahlias (or even cabbages), no immaculately trimmed privet hedge. Indeed, a van had been driven through the hallowed hedge and stood on what had once been assiduously mowed grass but was now a thicket of huge weeds. Bulging black plastic sacks littered the broken path round the side of the house, and the trellis that had been covered in climbing roses lay smashed on the ground. It looked as though it had been there many years, with half the wood buried in mud. All the curtains of the house were drawn though it was two in the afternoon. There was graffiti scrawled on the side wall in blue paint but most of it was obliterated by slashes of black.

The magazine had sent a photographer with me – there was always, in this series, a picture of the writer standing in front of the house. He said we should knock on the door – there was no bell – and just explain what we were doing. I was nervous about this. It wasn't part of the deal, as I had understood it. All I'd been asked to do, all I'd agreed to do, was write about my old life in the house. I'd heard stories of how the Raffles estate had now become a dangerous place, full of drug dealers, and from the look of Orton Road some of them might well be living here. A newspaper article had claimed, after all, that Raffles in Carlisle was on a par with Toxteth in Liverpool and the Broadwater estate in Tottenham. I really didn't want to disturb the inhabitants. But the photographer insisted we had to do it, and so I invited him to do it himself. I didn't see why he couldn't just take a quick snap, and then we could leave, sharpish.

He knocked. No response. He knocked harder, and for longer. Just as he was about to give up, and take the photograph anyway, a window on the upstairs floor was banged open and a furious woman's voice yelled, 'Who is it? What the fuck do you want? Fuck off!' The photographer bleated that he just wanted to

take a photograph of Margaret Forster, who once lived
here, for a feature about—. He was cut short. 'Do what
you fucking like but shut the fuck up,' shouted the
same furious voice, and the window was slammed shut
again. Was it any wonder that in the resulting picture
I looked tense and uneasy? I could hardly stand still,
never mind smile. All I wanted to do was leave quickly,
but, as is the way with colour magazine photographers,
one shot was not enough. On and on he went, having
me pose first in front of the door, then the downstairs
window, and just as he was moving me to the gate a
car screeched to a halt and a man got out of the front
passenger seat. He wasn't a big man, but he was burly
and he moved aggressively, pushing the gate open with
a force it didn't need, considering it was almost off its
hinges anyway. Before anything could be said by this
man, the photographer got in quickly, coming out with
the same patter he'd given the woman. The man
frowned, as though the photographer was speaking in
a foreign language and he had to translate it first before
he could decide what to do. I wondered if he would
ask for money, if he was someone who lived in the
house, for permission to take a photograph. Did he

41

have the right? Would the photographer give him a tenner? But it wasn't necessary. Just as abruptly as he'd arrived, the man left and, after he'd said something to the driver, the car swung round the corner into Dalton Avenue.

I've driven past the house since, but always rather quickly, and sadly. I thought I had no feeling for it whatsoever, that it didn't affect me in any way, but I found the dilapidation and neglect troubled me. It seemed to symbolise something distressing but I wasn't sure what – maybe just the shame that such a once aspirational building effort seemed to have ended like this. When, and why, had this utter change in Raffles come about?

At the time of that photograph, the house where I was born, and lived for fourteen years, looked condemned.

RICHARDSON STREET

Longsowerby
Carlisle

The council house we moved to in October 1952 faced Carlisle cemetery. It was at the top of a hill, near to the rather impressive entrance. At the bottom of this hill, there was a path which led through some open ground to the river Caldew, which meant we had easy access to a riverside walk all the way to Cummersdale. So, it was a pleasantly situated house, as long as being opposite a cemetery, and having hearses regularly pass by, wasn't found too depressing.

It didn't depress me in the least. I was familiar with the cemetery from an early age because my mother used to take me every week to tend her parents' grave. It was an outing I enjoyed. The cemetery was just a park to me, full of hidden paths criss-crossing between the grave-stones. It was beautifully maintained, with generous flower beds all along the main drive full of startlingly colourful bedding plants in the summer. There were poplar trees and fir trees mixed up with oak and ash trees, giving the whole place a deeply green appearance, and at the top, beyond all the rows of crosses for the war dead, there was a magnificent view of the fells. It seemed to me, as a child, quite a nice place to be dead in, if you had to be dead. I liked the jobs my mother gave me when we got to her parents' grave. The best one was being sent to get water from a nearby tank, to fill the metal holder in front of the white gravestone. We put flowers there every week, and the little bit of grass, surrounded by a white marble border, was carefully clipped by my mother. All around us, there would be other people doing the same, everyone intent on making graves as attractive as possible. My father thought this was morbid, but he had his own reasons for occasionally walking in the cemetery. He liked to pass his grandfather's grave, where his own name, Arthur Forster, attracted him. His grandfather's age, ninety, was a target he aimed at (he reached, and then passed it, dying at ninety-six). There were lots of other Forster graves I came to know as landmarks in the cemetery, though not so many on my mother's side, the Hinds. As far as I was concerned, the cemetery wasn't at all creepy. I was quite content to say that I lived opposite it. Looking out of our bedroom window, over its wall, at dead people, was fine by me.

The house itself was an undeniable improvement on the one we'd just left, but the condition it was in, was not. The inside was unbelievably dirty and dilapidated but there was no chance to do anything about this before we moved in and so we had to get cracking straight away, scraping the grime off the floors and walls, and scrubbing all the surfaces. The famous indoor lavatory, so longed for, took bottles of bleach and hours of repeated vigorous brushing before it was anything but disgusting. My mother, who of course had left Orton Road immaculate, was almost hysterical. Fastidious to a fault, it literally made her ill to be living in such a house, and she was the one living in it all the time while the rest of us escaped to work or school. It was a wet and cold October, making everything seem worse, and I dreaded those first few weeks, coming back to this house (though I never wished we were back in Orton Road, haven of cleanliness though it was).

Slowly, very slowly, the house was licked into shape, every wall painted or papered, my father doing all the decorating himself after his long shifts at the factory. After six months, there were so-called refinements taking place, some of which puzzled me. Doors, for example, which seemed fine to me. They were just wooden doors, four panels in each. But my mother wanted them 'flush'. This meant fitting a thin layer of plywood into the four panels so that the surface of the door was flat. I understood better her wish to be rid of the black range fireplace, the same sort we'd had in the Orton Road house. Black-leading the wretched thing went on being a nasty job, but it had to be done and it was my mother who did it. Funds wouldn't, as yet, stretch to having it removed and a modern fireplace put in.

Then, one day, my grandfather, George, arrived while my mother was doing this black-leading. He had taken to doing this since we arrived at the top end of his street (Richardson Street had privately owned houses at the bottom end and council houses on the hill after the road turned the corner). He didn't come to socialise. He came on the way back from visiting his wife's grave in the cemetery, and all he did was come in at the back door and stand there until my mother appeared and asked him if he'd like a cup of tea. She knew perfectly well he'd shake his head, or just grunt. There would be an awkward moment or two when, if he was in an expansive mood, he might make some comment on the weather – 'wet' – and then he'd turn and go. But this particular morning, when my mother didn't appear, he came into the house and saw her on her knees doing the black-leading. My mother said he just stood and stared, as ever saying nothing, then he left before she'd finished. He returned later that day. My father went to the door, hearing the latch being lifted, and came back with the startling news that a new fireplace had been ordered and would be put in the following week. It was something called an Osborne All-Tile fireplace complete with a steel grate. Oh, rapture! I was as thrilled as my mother. I'd never seen any beauty in the black range, which to me stigmatised the house. When the new fireplace arrived I was as admiring as everyone else, failing entirely to see how cheap and ugly it was.

The suspicion was growing that my grandfather was going soft in his old age. Arranging for a new fireplace to be put in could only be explained by what was obviously his regard for my mother. This regard was never expressed in words, and she'd been given no overt signs up to then that it existed, but it was surely there. His next act of uncharacteristic generosity couldn't be explained so easily.

He just made one of his unnerving appearances one day while I was sitting in the parlour with a board across my knees writing something for homework. He'd been brought in to admire my brother's handiwork (he'd built bookcases round the bottom part of the bay window). He said nothing, of course, but an instruction was (later) received to 'be in, Tuesday'. I was at school, but when I came home I was told by my smiling mother to 'go and look in the parlour'. Grandfather George had bought a bureau. It was no antique job, just a reproduction piece, but it was new and shiny, and had a leaf that let down so I could use it to do homework and lots of little cubby holes in which to keep pens and rubbers and paper clips. It set the tone for what this house, and this room, was to mean to me: a place of study.

What years those were, 1952–1956, each one heavy with ambition and determination to do well at school. Leaving school with my bike wobbling, the basket in front so weighed down with books, a girl once jeered:

'You're a swot!' and I nodded. Yup, I was a swot. A teacher had mentioned 'university' to me, and though I only had the vaguest idea what a university was, the thought of being able to leave home and go there appealed to me. I loved school, and university sounded like a sort of extended school, only with lots of other advantages. I was worried that going there must cost money and since I didn't have any, and my family certainly didn't (grandfather George's purse might stretch to fireplaces and bureaus, but, I imagined, that was the limit) I wouldn't be able to go even if I qualified, but it was explained to me that, with my father earning so little (though it wasn't put like that), I'd get a full grant. I might also be awarded a state scholarship. From then on, I was determined to go. All it was going to take was concentration and hard work.

There was no self-denial involved. I liked the studying. I didn't have to force myself in the least. Every evening, I sat in the parlour (it was always called that, never becoming a sitting room) and worked my way through homework, and then some extra reading. I didn't find the books I was reading myself. I had a teacher who fed me background reading, and who equipped me, at my request, with a long list of books a well-read person should've read. Until then, I'd been picking and choosing at random from the library shelves which was fine, up to a point, but now that point had been reached. It was lucky that, in this house, I had a room to study in and was no longer banished to a freezing bedroom. I actually had a fire there, a gas-fire in the corner, which spluttered and hissed alarmingly, its white tubes alternating between orange and red, but it gave out a good, if probably unhealthy, heat. I'd hear my father saying to my mother 'Has she got that fire burning money again?' but I was never told to turn it off.

I sat there long after I'd finished my famous studying, acting as though this was my own room. If any other family member dared to come in, I'd look indignant. Didn't they realise this room was dedicated to scholastic endeavour? What were they doing here? They'd come, sit in one of the two easy chairs, or stand looking out of the window, and then they succumbed to my silent glare and left the room. They were much more comfortable next door in the living room, I assured my guilty self, with a real fire on and the wireless, they didn't need to be in the parlour. Gordon didn't come in much, except occasionally to admire the bookshelves he'd made, which now held his collection of Book Club volumes he'd gathered while doing his National Service in the R.A.F. (I'd learned a lot from these books – one of them was Norman Mailer's *The Naked and the Dead*.) Mostly, though, he was rushing in and out of the house, working all day at a photographer's shop and taking wedding photographs at the weekends. It was Pauline who was next door with my parents, and she appeared, at that time anyway, to be quite content with their company. But my mother began to worry that it wasn't healthy for a teenage girl to be stuck in a room on her own reading for such long hours. I should be out. Out where? Just out, in the fresh air, but she didn't really mean I needed fresh air. She didn't *say* it wasn't normal for a girl my age, but that was what she meant. My answer was to take her literally. Fresh air? Right. I went out and walked in the cemetery for half an hour. Satisfied? Then I returned to the parlour. I wasn't after all going to be there for ever. Soon, I'd be leaving this house.

In my last summer there, things were a bit better. I took my books outside – plenty of fresh air – and sprawled on the minute patch of lawn allowed by my father, surrounded by the leeks and cauliflowers essential to feed the family. He'd worked hard on this garden, which had been in the same woeful state as the house. It was a huge improvement on Orton Road because it was all at the back and enclosed by a high hedge. There was still no real privacy but there was an illusion of it, and I was grateful for it. I was grateful, too, that we were in this house but somehow I wasn't grateful enough. I was greedy. I wanted more, specifically my own bedroom and bed, though I was at least realistic enough to realise it would be a long time before I ever had my own house. It had dawned on me that even some professional people couldn't afford to buy a house – teachers, for example. I'd somehow always thought teachers would be if not well off then certainly comfortably off, enough anyway to own a house. But one of our teachers at the High School had invited four of us home to look at some slides of her travels in France and Italy during the last summer holidays, and 'home' turned out to be a bed-sitting room in a house in Warwick Road. She'd been there years. It seemed to me inexplicable, but then I'd no idea how much a teacher earned or how much the cheapest house cost.

There was clearly a lot to learn about the economics of houses. The childish game of wandering down Norfolk Road and mentally occupying a house had stopped, but

I was still obsessed with the general unfairness of house ownership. What was needed, I decided, was a new law (not that I knew anything about the existing ones). This law would make it illegal for one person to live in a large house when big families were crammed into small ones. It was not fair, and it should be made fair, for everyone. This last bit, 'fair for everyone', troubled me. I saw difficulties. Would it be fair to turf my grandfather out of his house? He was seventy-six and had lived at 84 Richardson Street since he bought the house in 1920 while working as a mechanic at Pratchetts, a local engineering firm. Buying it had been a triumph, a real by-the-sweat-of-his-brow sort. I doubted if he had any affection for the house itself except that it was his, and this ownership signified a great deal. Its discomforts (many) didn't seem to worry him. He was used to them. He didn't mind still boiling water in a big, blackened kettle which hung on a hook over the fire so that he ran the risk of scalding himself every time he removed it to pour water into the waiting teapot. Apart from this fire, he had no other form of heating – quite normal for the times, or his times. But would my new imagined law make it right to move him out and a family in? No, of course not.

I couldn't kid myself. My grandfather's house was, I'm sure, full of painful memories for him, full of the sound of his wife lying for years in a bed in the corner of the living room, moaning with the pain of her rheumatoid arthritis (plus several other severe conditions). Wouldn't he want to escape from a house so filled with suffering? No. I knew that any suggestion of his house being taken from him would outrage him. He wouldn't even be interested in alternatives: somewhere smaller, warmer and cleaner? No! A home, perhaps, living companionably with others his own age. No! So, what was my proposed law to do about this problem? I toyed with the notion of getting the Queen to set an example by turning Buckingham Palace into flats, but even if she did this wasn't relevant to the problem of people like my grandfather. I just couldn't see how 'fair for everyone' could be made to work. It gave me a headache. Ambition to become a Member of Parliament and then Housing Minister faded. Houses were complicated; I wasn't up to tackling the rights and wrongs of ownership. My final thought, at that stage, was that nobody should be forcibly removed from their house if they had owned and lived in it for more than twenty-five years.

But what if they'd lived in it twenty-four years and six months?

I had other things to think about apart from the housing problem: Advanced Levels – the all-important A levels. Once they were over, in the summer of 1956, I emerged like a tortoise, slowly creeping into the kind of 'normal' social life my mother thought I should be enjoying. It wasn't that I'd been without friends all this time, but I'd never been part of a group doing the kind of things groups do. The group activity I got into the summer after A levels was fell walking. This was boy-led. We would set off on Friday evening, stay in a youth hostel, walk all the next day, stay in another youth hostel then come home. I loved it. The walking was often real climbing, and soon I'd climbed all the major fells in the northern lakes, rucksack on my back, and sampled every youth hostel from Keswick to Grasmere and Ullswater. I began to treat our house the way so many teenagers do, as a place to go and get a hot bath and good food, or, in other words, as a hotel which didn't charge. Sometimes we camped, and it nearly always rained, so coming back to our house then was even more appreciated. A house was a place full of material comforts, and that was all that mattered.

To some, it must have looked full of more comforts, in the way of possessions, than it actually was. We were burgled. All the burglar got was a few coins in a missionary box of my mother's, a little blue cardboard box with a slit in the top into which she slipped loose change now and again until it was full, when she handed it over to the vicar who passed it on to an appropriate society. The burglar had ripped the box open, easily done, pocketed the pennies, probably in disgust at how few there were, and thrown the box on the floor. He must quickly have realised there was obviously nothing of value, doubtless looking around in despair at the lack of jewellery or ornaments that might fetch a shilling or two. How many rooms he'd searched we never knew. Nothing, except that missionary box, was touched. He'd come in through the back door, which was on the latch (as most back doors were then, in our sort of houses). It had no bolt drawn across the top because the house wasn't unoccupied. I was in it, alone, asleep. Or, as my father, in a rage, put it later, 'We had a dog, but it never barked.'

It was so very rare for my parents not to be at

home in the evening. They'd gone out with my mother's sister, Aunt Nan, and Uncle Jack, and what may have given our burglar the wrong idea was that Jack had driven up in a Silver Cloud Rolls-Royce, and Nan was draped in a fox-fur stole. They were, by then, Jack having prospered, our well-off relatives and they'd come to take my parents out. My father, who loved cars but hated Jack, who flaunted his minor public school education and his new wealth, hadn't wanted to go, but allowed himself to be persuaded just so that he could experience the ride. They'd all come back apparently remarkably jolly (considering the tension that existed between my father and Jack) to find the front door wide open. My mother's first thought was for my safety so once she found me sound asleep, a book open on the pillow beside me, she accepted the loss of her missionary box money philosophically. My father didn't. He never believed for one moment that I'd been asleep, though I was very relieved that I really had been.

The burglar may, of course, have looked in on me, and perhaps got a fright, having believed the house was empty, so scarpered quickly. Or he may never have come up the stairs at all, one look having told him there were no rich pickings to be had. There were plenty of fingerprints when a bored policeman came to investigate, so the burglar hadn't thought to wear gloves. Probably just a lad, chancing it, was the opinion. But whoever this lad was, his little visit changed the feeling of the house. We'd been lucky – nothing really had been stolen, nothing harmed or wrecked – but the house no longer felt absolutely safe. A burglary was the kind of thing which might be expected to happen across the river Eden in Stanwix, or even in nearby Norfolk Road, but on the Longsowerby estate? What was the world coming to? There were limits, and they had just been broken. Afterwards, the nightly locking up took ages. If I came home later than 9 p.m. I had to give advance warning. If I didn't, back and front doors, sporting newly fixed bolts, would be found securely in place, defending the homeland.

Soon after this incident, my grandfather died, and his house, about which I'd worried so much, was put up for sale, the proceeds to be divided equally between my father and his younger brother, Bob. If this house had been a dismal place while still inhabited, it was twice as dreary and depressing now it was empty. I saw it after it was cleared of all the furniture and belongings – straight to the saleroom, nothing kept, not even the Crown Derby china I'd always ogled as it sat in its cabinet – and it was an almost frightening sight. The sun shone outside that day but very little sneaked into the rooms. The windows were still shrouded in net curtains, unwashed for a long time. Everywhere, the wallpapers were faded and discoloured, the paintwork chipped and worn. Where large pieces of furniture had been removed, it was a shock to see that what I'd thought a pattern of pale grey flowers mixed with darker grey ivy was once a pretty deep pink joined with a bright emerald green. What struck me, tiptoeing from room to room – the house seemed to demand a cautious tread – was that the place had no story to tell except one of neglect and exhaustion. The only atmosphere was one of a general decay. Whatever had happened in these rooms, nothing lingered. I knew some of the things that had happened – my brother's birth in the front bedroom, my grandmother's illnesses and her incarceration in the living room – but this didn't help bring the rooms alive. Mostly, there was a lingering feeling of unhappiness, but then perhaps most old houses, left in this state, feel that way.

It had always struck me as odd that my mother chose to give birth to her first child, my elder brother, in this house. Why didn't she have him at home, in her own house, in Orton Road? Or why not her mother's house? When asked, she said my grandmother Agnes so wanted her to have her first grandchild at *her* house that she had agreed. Agnes, at that time, was of course in good health and liked looking after people, whereas my maternal grandmother had a heart complaint. And Agnes, having no daughters, loved my mother and it was probably a way of showing her affection that she wanted to care for her during her 'lying-in'. Anyway, this was one happy event that had taken place, and I tried to imagine it as I took a last long look at that forlorn, shabby room, but my imagination for once failed me.

Viewers must have been as put off by the house as I was, because it took a long time to sell and when it did it was for far less than had been expected. My father, who was suddenly a firm believer in the law of primogeniture, was furious that the sum realised had, according to the terms of his father's will, to be split equally with his brother. It was wrong. He was the elder son and he should have the family house. By then, he and Bob had not spoken for eleven years. They both worked in the same factory, though Bob was a draughtsman while my father was a fitter, and they passed each other all the time without either brother giving any acknowledgement to the other. But quite apart from his being the elder, my father also reckoned he was entitled to the house because of the way he and my mother had looked after my grandmother. Who had come to the house three times a week to change her bedlinen and wash her? My mother. Who had brought her tasty home-baked scones and cakes? My mother. And where had Bob's wife been all this time? Nowhere near. Illness apparently upset her. And she 'wasn't too well' herself. My father was furious at what he perceived as rank injustice. It did no good. Bob got half. My father vowed he would never speak to him again but as he already hadn't spoken to him for so many years, the vow lost something of its force.

Houses, I now saw, could mean trouble. My father never tried to buy his own, but that was because he didn't have enough money, even with his share of his father's house, to buy one outright and he was afraid of taking a mortgage in case he couldn't keep the payments up. That, at least, was my reading of the situation, though I never asked him the reasons. Houses were too much of a sore subject. It came to my father's attention that Bob had bought a modern semi-detached house on London Road, to the south of Carlisle. Hearing this, presumably from workmates, my father cycled to London Road to look at Bob's house from the outside and came back announcing, contemptuously, that he didn't think much of it, and that Bob was 'trying to be something he's not'. I asked what that meant, and got only a withering look, so I cycled to London Road myself, only to remain baffled. There was nothing remarkable in any way about Bob's house. It was just ordinary, nothing flash, nothing about it was different from any of the scores of semi-detached houses being built at the time.

At any rate, no attempt, so far as I know, was ever made by my father to be something he was not. He went on renting our council house, improving it year by year to a considerable degree. Every now and again he would rage that I was doing nothing to help – '"Get a bigger house, and I'll help", she said'. I didn't remember saying this. He somehow implied that he'd moved us to an enormous mansion, with endless corridors and staircases as well as rooms, instead of to a house with one more bedroom and a parlour which took hardly any more effort to look after now that it was spick and span. And he himself, unusually for a working-class man of that era, did quite a lot of the housework. His speciality was vacuum cleaning (it was never called a Hoover). On Sunday mornings I'd waken to the horrible noise of the ancient vacuum cleaner being pushed round the carpet surrounding the bed. There was very little dirt or dust upon it, but on and on the noise would go, the vacuum cleaner pushed backwards and forwards remorselessly. If I groaned, he would say, 'Got to be done,' and carry on until the poor carpet was cleaned until it was threadbare.

My A level results came out in August 1956. They were good enough for me to be allowed to return to school to sit the Oxford and Cambridge entrance exams (at our school, this was how the system then worked). It was a big risk because if I failed to get a place I'd have wasted a year when I could already have been at a less prestigious university. And by then I had a distraction from my devotion to studying. I'd met, that summer, and become very involved with, a boy called Hunter Davies who was in his second year at Durham University . . . Maybe I should go to Durham. But I went ahead all the same and sat the exams. I got interviews at both Girton and Somerville, the first stage, but doubted if I'd negotiated either successfully. I was full of gloom by the time the telegrams came offering me an exhibition at Girton and a scholarship at Somerville. I don't remember feeling thrilled so much as relieved – taking those exams had seemed such a gamble and I'm not a gambler.

In March 1957, I left Richardson Street to go to Bordeaux, to be an au pair to a French family. It wasn't my idea, but I was charmed by it. The suggestion that I needed six months in France to improve my poor French was made by Somerville. I couldn't understand why, since I was to read history, I needed better French. I only hoped it didn't mean a lot of the history I'd be studying was going to be written in French.

I'd never, of course, been abroad, not that this was unusual in the 1950s. There'd been a school trip to Paris which I couldn't afford to go on, and was furiously jealous of those who could. Otherwise, I'd been no further south than Oxford and Cambridge, for interviews, so the thought of France, anywhere in France, was so exciting.

Our French teacher fixed up the au pair arrangement, and there was then an exchange of letters and photographs between me and the family. The snap of the five children I'd be helping to look after was taken in what was labelled 'the garden'. I naturally thought it was the family's garden. It looked promising, with lots of lawn and trees, surely the garden of a big house. I didn't realise 'garden' in this case meant Public Park, and that the family, in fact, had no garden or any kind of outside space. The number of children – the eldest seven, the youngest eighteen months – daunted me, but I was assured I'd have every afternoon off and I'd have my own room. My parents had no part in these arrangements. My mother was worried about me going so far away to a foreign country, but she was also quite impressed, and my father thought there was 'no need' for it, and 'no point' in going to Oxford either, but he didn't interfere. I was given up as lost, definitely trying to be something I was not.

After these six months, I'd be leaving again to go to Oxford, so even though I might have to come back for some vacations for the following three years, this leaving to go to Bordeaux was the real breakaway. I was well aware of it. I couldn't wait to get away from this house. I thought

– consciously thought – goodbye dreary cramped bedroom, goodbye poky parlour where I'd spent so many hours hunched over biographies and history books, goodbye to all that. I already, in my mind's eye, saw myself in my very own room in Bordeaux, conjuring up a romantic vision of 'the garden' I'd be looking out over, and the bright blue continental sky with the sun always shining. Looking around for what felt like the last time, I felt already that I'd never lived here. There wasn't a trace of me hanging about. The walls couldn't speak, they had absorbed nothing of me, but then how could they have done. I'd just passed through this house – that was all.

But coming back six months later, it surprised me how differently I regarded it. In Bordeaux, the family I lived with had three rooms, four flights of stairs up above a newsagent's shop. There was no bathroom – 'all-over washes' were the order of the day, and they took place at the sink on the landing, which served also as a kitchenette. The lavatory made me wonder why on earth I'd resented the outside lavatory at Orton Road which, I now saw, was luxurious. What the family had was the typical French variety meaning not a flush toilet but one with a metal platform inside the bowl which, when lifted by a handle at the back, dropped anything deposited down a chute. I didn't like to enquire exactly what happened when waste got to the bottom. I did, as promised, have my own room but it was not the room I'd imagined. No window, for a start, only a skylight, and this might have been romantic but it wasn't. The skylight didn't open, and the room was stifling. Mice scurried about all night, and the mattress was infested with fleas. I learned later from a relative of the family that three previous au pair girls from England had left within days.

I did, though, see another side of how some of the French lived. The grandfather lived in a beautiful house, with a balcony, in a leafy street, and another relative not only had what I thought of as a proper mansion but also a beach house on the nearby coast. My host family, surprisingly, also had a country cottage among the pine woods at Salaunes, not far from Bordeaux. It was primitive – cooking was on an open fire, the water obtained from a well, and the only lavatory was the woods. But it was the definition of 'picturesque', built of stone with a tiled roof (holes in it, but still . . .) and framed by trees, some of them cherry trees which were laden with fruit. It was straight out of a fairy story and I loved it there, expecting either Hansel or Gretel to appear at any moment.

I ought, always, to have seen the merits of Richardson Street, considering I'd already had my aunts' flats to compare it with, but somehow I hadn't appreciated the sheer luxury of living in a whole house, whatever the house was like, till I went to France. It did me a lot of good, being an au pair in such circumstances, doing a great deal more than improving my French. It made me finally ditch my snobbery about houses, just in time, before I went to Oxford where, to my astonishment, living in a council house was apparently a source of wonder.

WINCHESTER ROAD

Oxford

My room in Somerville College was in the library block, built in 1903 along the northern perimeter of the grounds. Somerville wasn't ancient, like the men's colleges, so many of them possessing 'dreaming spires', but it was imposing enough for me.

I had a corner room with a mullioned window overlooking a lawn and a cedar tree. It was a peaceful, pleasant view. I could sit in the window seat and read and watch undergraduates coming and going. The room was square and large and sparsely furnished with a bed, a table, two chairs and a bookcase, all well worn. It was roughly three, maybe four, times the size of our living room at home, and I struggled to fill it. My stuff looked not just lost in it but wrong. The cups and saucers I'd bought in Woolworths looked ridiculous in that setting – I should have had my grandmother's Crown Derby – and even the modern kettle I'd been so pleased with looked ludicrous. I'd brought two Picasso posters, but I didn't put either of them up. The room would've screamed. I could see that this room was, in fact, quite shabby, but its very shabbiness was somehow grand. I felt aware, all the time, of those who had gone before me, fitting comfortably into a place probably not dissimilar to their room at home, though there was no obvious trace of these women. The carpet, of indeterminate colour and pattern, bore the marks of many feet, and the bedspread was frayed through use. The table had had ink spilled on the surface, and when I looked closely, I could see scratches – initials – along the rim, which I couldn't quite make out.

Outside my room there was a door leading from the main part of the college to the library. The slap of the door opening and shutting, and the sound of voices as people swept through it, disturbed the otherwise intense hush. I supposed I would get used to the noise outside, the ebb and flow of the human traffic, but I never quite did. It was a constant reminder that I was living in a community even if I did have, at last, a room of my own. But that was the trouble. It didn't feel at all like my own. It felt like somebody else's. I felt, increasingly, as though someone was watching me, breathing down my neck, asking what I thought I was doing here. How foolish, to imagine this could ever be *my* room.

It didn't take me long to discover that living in a college didn't suit me. Somerville was an attractive college to live in, the atmosphere pretty free and easy, but I just didn't like being surrounded by other people though many of them were now my friends. It was the sheer noise I disliked. The common room didn't appeal either, in spite of the comfortable sofas and all the magazines and newspapers. It always seemed to be full of braying voices discussing their own opinions. I wasn't in the least intimidated by this type of girl, but I didn't like their company. This reaction to college life was all a shock to me. I'd always fantasised about going to boarding school, the sort of school featured in Angela Brazil stories, and I'd imagined a college to be a blissful version of this which I would immediately love. Instead, I longed to escape, so very early in that first year I started plotting to move out of college in my second year.

I knew this would be thought odd, maybe even suspicious. I had the privilege, as a scholar, of being able to stay in college the whole three years, whereas others had to move into lodgings at the end of the first. Why did I want, voluntarily, to go into lodgings? What was the motive? Saying that college life didn't suit me sounded vaguely insulting, and considering I had a choice room it seemed ungrateful. But I was listened to with patience and at last, with some reluctance, I was given permission to look for lodgings, though these, of course, had to be on the college's approved list. I didn't find them myself. One of my friends, Theodora, found the two rooms we were to rent. They had been let to undergraduates for the last decade, though only lately to women. The house in Winchester Road was a small nineteenth-century terraced cottage in a quiet area round the corner from a line of shops called North Parade. It was only a ten-minute walk from Somerville, where we would still be having our meals. We went to look at it, and to be looked at, by the landlady.

Mrs Brown was sitting in her front room waiting to receive us. She was straight out of Jane Austen, wearing a little lace cap on her white hair and a shawl round her shoulders. She sat very upright and peered at us through her wire-rimmed spectacles. She had a slightly regal air which seemed somehow affected, yet it never slipped, and she had perfected a gracious nod of reply to anything said to her, so that it was impossible to tell if she had actually heard. Mr Brown, we assumed, must be dead. He was never mentioned, not even as 'my late husband' and Mrs Brown referred to 'my' house all the time. She had rules, which we eagerly agreed to, none of them at all troublesome. She then spent quite a lot of time boasting about the 'young gentlemen' who had been her lodgers in previous years, one of whom was, she told us, now famous. We had never heard of him, but pretended we had, and expressed our admiration. Then Mrs Brown dismissed us, with a slight wave of her hand, into the care of her sister Fanny, who would show us the rooms.

Fanny was different, very different. She was small, under five feet, and plump, with wild, white hair pushed back from her face, and she smiled all the time. Whereas Mrs Brown was elegantly, if quaintly, dressed, Fanny wore a white apron over a blue dress which reached almost to her heavy, black shoes. Her accent was different too. Fanny had a broad country accent, not quite West Country but near to it, and Mrs Brown a refined accent (though she spoke so slowly that this was perhaps acquired). Fanny, who was all friendliness, chattering away and addressing us as Miss Margaret and Miss Theodora, showed us the two rooms we were to have, one at the front of the first floor of the house, one at the back. The front room was much larger than the back one. It looked out on to the little front garden where roses grew in a ragged, chaotic way round a tiny bit of grass. This room had a gas fire and a gas ring big enough to balance a pan upon it, so if we wanted we might manage to cook scrambled eggs, or at least make cocoa. This was to be Theo's room (she, after all, had found these rooms). The back room, mine, was less than half the size and looked out on to a yard but it had a real fire which I was told I could use if the weather was exceptionally cold.

I loved Winchester Road from the moment we moved in. It was an odd set-up, but we fitted in surprisingly quickly. Mrs Brown sat in her front room all day, with Fanny coming and going in answer to the rap of her walking stick on the floor. Fanny never sat down, so far as we could tell. She did all the work in the house, commenting loudly on whatever she was doing, often with what sounded like resentment towards her sister – 'sweep the hall floor, she says, as if it wasn't damned well swept already'. It was impossible to believe that Mrs Brown and Fanny really were sisters since they were so unalike in every respect, and though this is familiar enough in many families there seemed an extra strangeness about this relationship. It was no good being inquisitive – even the most harmless questions were turned aside by Fanny – but though she appeared to be fond of us, I don't think she really was. She muttered to herself when she thought we were out of hearing, and some of these mutterings revealed the same sort of suppressed fury she harboured towards her sister – 'won't be long in the bathroom, they say, won't be long, what's nearly an hour, an hour, and all the hot water used, damned more than won't be long . . .'. We tried very hard to keep on the right side of Fanny, aware that it was she, not Mrs Brown, who really ran the household.

There was also a third person living there: Reg. We never knew his surname. Just as Mrs Brown was always Mrs Brown, Reg was always Reg, and his relationship to both these women went unexplained. Fanny bossed him around, treating him with what would often sound near to contempt. Reg never reacted. He was an elderly man, we reckoned about seventy but, of course, we were going on appearances and to nineteen-year-olds he looked ancient. We may have been misled by his shaggy white moustache and sparse white hair and his old-fashioned, much-worn clothes. He wore loose grey flannel trousers, much too big for him, held up by a belt with a snake fastening on it, and a brown tweed jacket with leather patches on the elbows. He also wore a tie, striped red and black with something, some emblem, repeated between the stripes. It was no good trying to ask him about this tie, or anything else, because he was terrified of us. If we met him in the hall – though the passageway was hardly a hall – he'd panic at our 'Hello, Reg!' and flatten himself against the wall until we'd sailed past. He shuffled round the house all day, with Fanny bawling at him to 'bring the damned coal in', or 'get on with them potatoes.' Doing these jobs meant, we thought, that Reg could not be a 'paying guest', but if he wasn't a lodger, what was he?

Another of his jobs was to look after the garden. This was definitely his favourite occupation. It got him away from Fanny, and he made sure that this gardening took him a long time. He'd stand with a pair of secateurs in his hands observing the overgrown borders and then after a great deal of apparent thought he'd choose one rose and clip round it. I thought he was pruning, but it was hard to tell when the clipping seemed so random. Mowing the lawn was another task he devoted himself to. This lawn was a mere six feet by nine feet. He had one of those simple mowing machines which make such a soothing, gentle rushing noise as they go backwards and forwards, and Reg loved both the sound and the minimal effort needed. It was a job that required only five minutes once a week, but Reg made it last half an hour and would have done it every dry day if Fanny hadn't yelled at him to stop that damned mowing again.

Reg, like Mrs Brown, never seemed to leave the house. The highlight of his week was Saturday evening when he went up to the attic where he slept and after a bit of shuffling about we'd hear a rhythmic pounding of his feet as he sang 'Yo ho ho and a bottle of rum!' Did he have a bottle of rum? We hoped so, though if Mrs Brown had known she would have had him out of the house at once, so strong was her antipathy to alcohol – 'strong drink is wicked and leads to evil' she'd told us, as she'd warned us not to bring it into her house. We didn't know if Fanny heard Reg, but it seemed unlikely when he was so far above her quarters.

What exactly these quarters consisted of, we never knew because we were never allowed in them. There was a door, next to the door which led into Mrs Brown's sitting room, which we used to go and knock on if we wanted to ask Fanny something. She'd come out and stand with her back to the door while she talked to us, never allowing us to glimpse the room beyond. But there must have been more than one room. I could see from my bedroom window that there was a back addition to the house, so I reckoned there was a kitchen and another room at least. Fanny must have slept in this other room, but that left Mrs Brown. Where did she sleep? With Fanny? It was hard to credit, knowing the gulf she liked to keep between herself and her sister.

The rooms Theo and I had would obviously have been the bedrooms in the house, and I wondered if giving them up to lodgers had been a decision Mrs Brown had been forced to make for economic reasons. After all, what other reasons could there have been? Perhaps, in spite of her carefully cultivated gentility, she had no other income. It probably helped that no money actually changed hands. The college did the paying, so the pretence that we were 'guests' was maintained easily. Certainly none of the money was spent on the house itself. Everything was clean and neat, kept so by Fanny's labours, but the walls and paint-work hadn't been touched for a long time, and the stair carpet was worn. The tread of our own feet, plus that of our many friends, wore it out even more, though Fanny didn't seem to hold this against us. She was particularly interested in what she called our 'gentleman callers', though they were just friends, some of whom took the time and trouble to ingratiate themselves with her. They may have thought themselves successful, and believed the chuckling Fanny loved them, but she muttered about them afterwards just as she muttered about us – 'looking blooming, am I, and what do you want, smarming me'. She let them come and go after hours, but made it clear Mrs Brown must never find out. A lot of tiptoeing went on, and lots of winks and fingers-to-lips from an (apparently) gleeful Fanny.

It was perhaps a kind of contradiction, that I loved that house and my room in it. It was extremely small, and since I'd complained for years about feelings of claustro-phobia at home you'd have thought I'd have felt this even more strongly here. But I didn't. There was barely room to move, with a bed, a chest of drawers, a small table and a chair filling the space, but I thought it snug, not cramped. This, I felt, had always been a woman's room, though I based this feeling on the evidence alone of the wallpaper, a rose pattern on a cream (or once cream) background, and the curtains, also a washed-out rose-patterned cotton. I asked Fanny once if it had ever been her bedroom. She didn't reply, just ignored the question, but her expression suggested she was quite shocked at the idea, though I couldn't think why.

She often put her head round the door when I was in my room, ostensibly to tell me something there was no need to tell because she'd told me already, and I knew she was checking that I hadn't taken down the net curtain shrouding the lower part of the window. This was not allowed. It was there 'for decency', and if Mrs Brown discovered it had been removed she, Fanny, would be 'for it'. It was no good arguing that there wasn't any need to worry about this 'decency' because no one could see in anyway, so I just pulled the net to one side, to let in more light, and Fanny let this pass.

Inside the cupboard, where I hung my clothes, there were some coat hangers covered in pretty material and with a little lavender bag attached. The scent of lavender had long since faded but if the cupboard was closed all day and then opened there was a faint trace of it, just the merest whiff, and then it was gone. I imagined the dresses which had once hung there, the sprigged cottons, the fine muslins . . . but more likely the drab grey and brown of servants' dresses. I imagined more than the dresses. It was the sort of room that nurtured and encouraged the imagination, especially with the fire lit, flickering away and creating those shadows which could be turned so easily into people. Lying in bed on a winter's night with just the bedside lamp on – it had a pale pink silk shade which, just like the net curtain, could not be changed – that room wrapped itself round me as securely as the old-fashioned eiderdown. The atmosphere was always, on these nights, gentle and soothing, but as the fire burnt itself out it became more mysterious, not so innocent. If I'd believed in ghosts, that is when I could have convinced myself the room was suddenly crowded with them, all women or girls, sighing their way to my bed, their long hair unbraided, their white nightdresses catching the dying light of the fire's embers . . . I'd grow dangerously sentimental before I fell asleep.

I never knew how much the house in Winchester

Road was worth, but made the mistake of thinking that as it was small, and not in good condition, it might, one day, be within what I hoped would be my means to buy it. I thought I could definitely live there (with Mrs Brown, Fanny and Reg ejected, of course, in another of my merciless fantasies). I didn't long for the Edwardian villas of Carlisle's Norfolk Road any more – too big, too lacking in the charm of Winchester Road, which I now recognised. I fancied myself by then a good reader of the character of houses, though if asked I doubt if I could have defined what I meant in this instance by 'character'. I'd been in a good few houses during my three years at Oxford, including some in London, where friends lived. Size, I'd learned, was not everything. You could get lost in some of these houses, and they could be exhausting, with so many stairs and so many hidden rooms at the end of corridors which made no immediate sense. I certainly didn't yearn for a 'cosy' house, in spite of my love of Winchester Road, but I saw the drawbacks of 'rambling' too. I sometimes could hardly grasp that one family could inhabit the five floors of a Notting Hill mansion and apparently hardly notice. There were rooms, more than one, which were libraries, shelves and shelves of books with more piled on tables and the floor, and others that appeared to be solely for music, with a piano in the centre and a cello in the corner. I didn't know how, whatever life I was going to lead, I could ever cope with the opportunities of such a house.

There was another house I was invited to, in the Cotswolds, which was a shock in another way. I'd been told it was a cottage, so I imagined it would be like Winchester Road, but with a good garden and standing on its own, not in a terrace, and maybe (I did hope so) with a thatched roof. It did have a thatched roof but there the resemblance to any cottage I'd ever seen ended. It was such a beautiful house, only one storey, but with eight rooms stretching over a large area and surrounded by a huge garden which had a pond full of water lilies and a gazebo and stone steps leading down to a tennis court. I fell silent. It was too much to absorb this 'cottage'. All the way back to Winchester Road I was wondering if I could ever live in such a perfect house and surprising myself by deciding no, I didn't think I could. It was too much, I wouldn't be up to owning such an impressive house. Clearly, choosing a house, when the time came, was going to be much more complicated than I'd ever expected. There were so many aspects to take into consideration. How a house *felt* was as important as how it looked.

But buying a house wasn't a privilege I was going to have for many more years. There were other more important things to think about as we approached finals, such as careers. What was so urgent about having a house? It was materialistic, worthless as an ambition. Houses were places of shelter, that was all, and had no significance in themselves, surely. A roof, four walls, bricks and mortar – nothing to get excited about. Being *free* of property was preferable. But not to me. I worried more about where I was going to live than what job I was going to have, though at least I could see these two things were closely related and interdependent. Surroundings had always mattered to me. Whatever work I was going to do, coming home to somewhere I hated would result in my working less well – a high-and-mighty deduction which didn't bear examination, it was so silly.

I was married from Winchester Road on 11th June 1960, disappointing Fanny by not looking as a bride should. No long, white dress and veil, no bouquet, no grand car, with white ribbons streaming from it to carry me to the church. No church either. We were married at the register office in St Giles with Theo and Mike, an old friend from Carlisle, as witnesses. My belongings had already been packed and despatched, for the moment, back to Carlisle, and I'd said goodbye to Mrs Brown, Fanny and Reg. Fanny even managed a few tears, though what exactly provoked them I'm not sure (maybe disappointment that I wasn't having a 'real' wedding rather than because she was sad to see me leave).

Already, that day in June 1960, when I left Winchester Road, that house had started to become a memory, its influence upon me not at all easy to decide. Quite quickly, its hold on me started to lose its power, so much so that I became unsure why I'd loved it in the way I had. I tried to cling on to the feelings my little room had given rise to, the sense of security and calm it seemed filled with. And then, of course, there had been many happy hours there, sneaking Hunter in (Theo sneaked her man in too) while Fanny pretended not to be aware of what was going on. That room was the first place we had any privacy (Somerville was never guaranteed private, though women managed, and men had to be out by 7.30 p.m.). Previous to that, in Carlisle, we had never had a room. Hunter, when at home during the university vacations, lived on a council estate, St Anns Hill. His house was much more crowded than ours. His father, who had MS, was, by the time I came on the scene, mostly confined to bed in their equivalent of our parlour. His twin sisters had one of the bedrooms, his mother another, and he shared the other with his younger brother. When he was at Durham, a lodger took his place, and was often still there in vacations. So, no privacy there, and none of the sort we wanted at my house. On wet, cold evenings, we took long bus rides on the top deck, which was often empty before it reached the terminus. Winchester Road had given us a whole, warm room to ourselves, with no danger of parents or siblings bursting in.

But I knew I'd just been an interloper in the house's history (which I didn't even know). Theo and I passed through it, gone in a flash, like so many other undergraduates. Probably in a couple of years Fanny would have difficulty remembering our names when she had a whole sequence of names to recall. I never went back, but then

I didn't go back to Oxford until twenty-eight years later, and then only for the day.

We were going to live in London, but, thank God, not in the flat my husband had been living in and which I'd thought might be my unwelcome fate. That flat was in Kingscroft Road, Kilburn, and I'd spent a long vacation there and hated it, swearing melodramatically that it would make me ill to have to live there when we were married. The flat was on the top floor of an ugly semi-detached house in a dreary road off Kilburn High Road. It consisted of two rooms – plus tiny kitchenette and bathroom – squashed under the roof. That's how it felt to me, squashed, compressed, barely able to breathe, the insubstantial walls squealing with the effort of staying upright. It was let as a furnished flat and this furniture was hideous, as was the decor, all large patterns and garish colours. The windows were tiny and impossible to open more than an inch, and there was a smell about the house the moment the front door, shared with the other occupants, was opened. It wasn't a bad smell, just a fusty one, as though the house belonged to an elderly aunt who had recently died and nobody had yet cleared her stuff out. But if I detested this perfectly adequate flat so much, it was up to me to find an alternative before our wedding day.

So I did, through friends of Theo's. The day we were married, we went not to Kingscroft Road but to Heath Villas, Hampstead.

HEATH VILLAS

Vale of Health
Hampstead
London

London, everyone knew, was a huge city, crowded with buildings and endless streets so that the idea there might exist a 'heath' within its outer boundaries was, I thought, a nonsense. 'Heath' meant a wild space, a mixture of rough ground and trees and bushes. This 'Hampstead Heath' must just be some sort of park, and the 'Vale of Health' not a 'vale' at all but a romantic misnomer for what was probably a miserable little square of grass. The reality amazed me. Coming from Spaniards Road down a narrow path the Heath turned out to be indisputably a heath, stretching as far as the eye could see over the thickets of bushes and trees, and there at the foot of this path, was what could genuinely be described as a vale, a dip surrounded by greenery. I'd never imagined anything like it could exist so close to the centre of a capital city.

Heath Villas was not as old as other houses in the vale. Numbers 1–6 were built in 1862; 7–12, round the corner, were built in 1868. They were all Victorian terraced houses, with a basement and then three floors above, and numbers 7–12 backed on to a pond. By the end of the nineteenth century, there were fifty-three houses in this vale, and what was once an area of bog had become a most desirable address. There was only one road leading into it, and one short road leading off that in turn, but there were little paths, cuts, connecting the various cottages. Opposite the house in which we hoped to rent a flat, there was a triangular patch of ground surrounded by railings, which appeared to protect nothing more precious than a couple of spindly trees and some bushes. This was the centre of the vale, if it could be said to have a centre at all.

What it had in abundance was an association with lots of famous names. The blue plaques were everywhere. That first time we went there, it was D.H. Lawrence's name that sprang out from all the others. He'd lived, though not for long, at 1 Byron Villas, on the short stretch of road leading to the fairground and the pub. It seemed so odd that there was still this area, on the edge of the vale, devoted to an annual fair, and here a few caravans stood all the year round. The huge Victorian pub was another surprise – why such a pub for so few houses? The more we traced the outline of the vale, the odder and more mixed-up it seemed. It wasn't like any place I'd ever imagined living in.

But we weren't living there yet. The couple who were, friends-of-friends of Theo's, explained that we would have to be vetted by the landlord, a Mr Elton. He was, they said, very nice but a little eccentric, with a phobia about noise. He lived at Heath Villas, on the top floor, and the basement and half of the ground floor were let to an elderly woman. The couple emphasised how inconveniently arranged their flat was, with the bedroom on the ground floor, next to the elderly lady's sitting room, and the kitchen and living room on the next floor with the shared bathroom up again from that, on the half landing. Also, the flat was unfurnished, so we would have to bring our own furniture. I don't think I was listening properly to any of this because I'd already decided I loved the flat and the vale and was determined to live there.

The living room was a particularly attractive room, with two large sash windows looking out into the centre of the vale. The kitchen, opening off it, overlooked the pond and beyond the pond there was what seemed a never-ending vista of trees, not a man-made thing in sight. The bedroom, it was true, was awkwardly placed and small, with barely space for a double bed and a chest of drawers, and the view here was of a yard, rather like Winchester Road. But that didn't matter. Nothing mattered, except to secure this flat. A meeting was arranged with Mr Elton. I'd already imagined him as a kind of Reg figure, though tidier and better educated. He was a civil servant, and turned out to look how I'd thought a civil servant would look (never having met one in my life), which is to say neatly dressed, in a dark suit, bald, bespectacled and slight in build. He seemed nervous and hesitant, which was unexpected, considering he had all the power. As he asked us questions, he rubbed his hands together a lot, and blinked rapidly, never looking straight at either of us.

It emerged, eventually, that there were three things about us which concerned him. One, our youth: we were twenty-two and twenty-four, and he felt that no couple in their twenties could possibly be as quiet as he wanted his tenants to be. Without openly criticising them, he implied that the current tenants (the friends-of-friends of Theo, who were in their early thirties) had most certainly not been quiet enough, though the examples he mentioned – including the banging of doors – didn't seem too heinous. He made it clear that he would not tolerate *any* noise after ten o'clock at night, not even the noise of a lavatory being flushed (if used after ten, the lid should be put down and the first person using it in the morning would know to flush it). His second worry was what kind of financial backing we had. This was tricky. Of course, we had none. The delicate enquiries about our fathers' employment soon revealed this, and it was only Hunter's job as a journalist which went some way to reassuring him. I said I intended to get a job as soon as I graduated, so we would have two incomes and would be able to afford the six guineas a week comfortably. This brought him to his third concern, though he was such a shy, easily embarrassed man that he struggled to express it: children. He would not allow children because of the unavoidable noise. Once we'd sensed what he was hinting at, we said we didn't want children yet either, not for years, though we didn't point out that we'd successfully avoided having any for quite a long time already, feeling this would be a bit too much information for him. Finally, he said he'd think about it, and let us know. I went back to Oxford and wrote to him, thanking him for the meeting, and enthusing about his house, ending by saying that even if he decided we were not suitable tenants I would never forget his house and how much I loved it. A bit gushing, but I meant it.

Mr Elton said yes, we could rent his flat, with a trial period of three months and, if satisfactory, a lease afterwards of three years. Hunter moved in on 1st June, and we arrived there as a married couple soon afterwards.

Our flat, when we moved in, seemed even lovelier, now that it was empty of furniture, especially the main room. The fitted carpet there was a pale green, the walls white, and the large windows let in the sun through a latticework of leaves. It felt so airy, so spacious, the spirits lifted just to walk into it. The kitchen was equally cheering, the view of the pond dominating the whole room. The previous tenants had left an old deal table here, for which we were grateful, and two stools, and we had bought their cooker from them, quite enough to start us off. It would have been nice to have a fridge, but we needed a bed more, our first purchase.

So that was it. By the end of June 1960, we were settled in our first home, except it didn't yet feel like 'home'. On the contrary, it felt strange, if delightfully so. We didn't know the house itself, or our section of it. Coming back to it each day was a shock for many weeks. Walking down the winding road that led from East Heath Road into the Vale felt as mysterious as it had when we discovered it. It was like entering a secret hideout for which we might need a password (and cynics might say that password was 'money' – the houses were all expensive either to buy or rent). I felt ridiculously pleased to be able to walk up the steps to the yellow door of our house in Heath Villas and to own a key which opened it. It was so peaceful once inside the house that the merest creak going up the stairs sounded explosive and I soon learned to avoid the sixth stair, the one which had a loose board under the carpet.

Our flat, or two rooms of it, had a door on the landing, cutting it off from the staircase, so that once inside it felt self-contained. We never heard Mr Elton, above us, or Mrs Woodcock, the tenant in the flat below. The house, it was easy to pretend, belonged entirely to us. They were both as respectful of our privacy as we were of theirs, and in no time at all we were comfortable with each other. Mr Elton was particularly pleased that Mrs Woodcock approved of us. We never discovered how the two of them came to be friends, or how Mrs Woodcock came to be living in his house, but he always seemed just slightly wary of her. If Mrs Brown, back in Winchester Road, had given the impression of aping gentility, there was no doubt that Mrs Woodcock was the real thing. She was a rather haughty, dignified, elderly woman, always well dressed, with coiffured white hair, slow in her movements but not because of any disability. She was unfailingly polite and gracious, but she had a sharp tongue if disagreed with which she didn't hesitate to use. It would've been easy to be intimidated by her.

We received a note, left for us on the hall table, in our first week there, inviting us for sherry at 5.30 p.m. one day. We both went, but after that first time it was usually just me, because Hunter would still be at work. It became an established routine that twice a week I would go down to Mrs Woodcock's sitting room and take sherry, poured into exquisite crystal glasses, the sort to be sipped from slowly. Mrs Woodcock suited the house. She might not have been the owner but she looked, and sounded, as though she was, sitting in her Queen Anne armchair with a slightly imperious air. What contrasted with this impression of being above everyone and everything was her genuine curiosity. She was keen to know about us, but held back from asking direct questions because to do so was, in her opinion, impertinent. Information, which she badly wanted, had to emerge gradually without seeming to have been requested. It was a good game, which I played cunningly once I'd recognised it as such. We didn't chat, we conversed. I noticed that I became affected by Mrs Woodcock's ultra-correct speech. Careless grammar irritated her. She never said so, but if I came out with slang, she winced slightly, and so I tried to speak properly. There was no cut-and-thrust of real debate either, no interrupting Mrs Woodcock's speech as ideas occurred to me. If I did cut in, knowing what she was going to say because it had become obvious and she was being long-winded, when I'd made my point she would simply resume, where I had made her leave off.

But she did like to be challenged. The subjects we

ranged over were usually chosen by her, and at first it was like a stately game of tennis. She would lob a question about the matter she'd decided on, often political, in such a way that it could be easily answered, but then she would direct another, tempting me to return it with vigour. She was quite pleased if we then had a disagreement, and would smile as though she had won a point by provoking me. Her standards of morals and behaviour were high, and she expected others to adhere to them. Vulgarity, or what she termed vulgarity, in particular offended her, and what she considered vulgar could seem to me simply funny. The *Sunday Times* colour magazine's first issue was an example. The day it was delivered, I saw her hold it in a pair of sugar tongs and ostentatiously drop it into the dustbin, turning her head away as if she was holding a rotten, stinking fish.

I think Mr Elton was relieved that Mrs Woodcock seemed to like us because it took some of the responsibility to be sociable off him. Why he felt he ought to be sociable I don't know, but he clearly did. She tried to boss him about, and though he would agree with what she told him needed to be done, about house, he didn't always do it, or not until it suited him. He also didn't like being drawn in any way into looking after her when she was not feeling well, which was where I came in useful. She had a son, and also a niece, and she sometimes wanted them to be called upon to do something for her but she wanted this obligation to be made clear to them by someone else. I didn't like doing it, but I allowed her to enlist my help, and would agree to ring either the son or the niece and say I'd found their mother, or aunt, in rather a bad way, feeling breathless, and I just thought they would want to know . . . they didn't in the least want to know, and deeply resented my do-gooder calls, but usually they came, and that would satisfy Mrs Woodcock for a while. Mr Elton was very glad to be excused this sort of chore.

He came to our flat, very occasionally, for a drink, though Mrs Woodcock never did, in spite of repeated invitations. She claimed that the stairs were too steep, and refused all help to manage them, but I think the truth was that she always preferred to be on her own ground. Anyway, there would have been nowhere for her to sit except for the stools in the kitchen. We hadn't yet got any easy chairs, just some big cushions. We'd got it into our heads that a gracious room like our sitting room needed gracious furniture, and we trawled through antique shops in Camden Town, trying to find it at a price we could afford. We were probably influenced by Mrs Woodcock, who held modern furniture in contempt, especially any betraying a Scandinavian influence. When we finally bought two second-hand wing chairs, poor copies of her genuine Queen Anne, she was rather approving as she saw us carrying them in. Battered though they were, and mere imitations, they were not 'modern junk'. We quickly found out that modern junk might have been a lot more comfortable.

Her influence extended into other areas too. The first time I had sherry with her, she said I would need the telephone number of her greengrocer, butcher and fishmonger so that I could place my order and it could be delivered at the same time as hers. The thought of having an order had never entered my head, but I was quite charmed with the idea. Perhaps living in this house required such behaviour. Mrs Woodcock pointed out that the walk from even the nearest shop was a long way, and that carrying heavy bags would be bad for my back, best to be sensible. I thought I'd try it, and solemnly rang up, as instructed, and read out what

I thought amounted to 'an order'. Gosh, it was jolly good fun – I felt I was in a radio play, or maybe *Mrs Dale's Diary* (a popular soap). A van from each of the various establishments duly arrived, and I tripped down the steps, ever so ladylike, to collect my order. I committed, what in Mrs Woodcock's opinion was, a faux pas by paying in cash there and then, when the done thing, as I should have known, was to have an account. The fruit, the vegetables, the meat and the fish were all of excellent quality but they were also, of course, extremely expensive. I never had an order delivered again, as Mrs Woodcock undoubtedly noticed, though no comment was made.

She was quite right, though, about the long walk from the shops. It took me a while to work out the best way to get to and from the High Street with so many different routes available and all of them interesting to walk along. Hampstead was such an unusual area, full of contrasts everywhere, with large houses mixed up with little terraces of cottages, and all kinds of narrow passageways connecting the broad roads. It was all uphill and downhill, with views of the Heath appearing suddenly at almost every corner. I learned more about houses, just walking through Hampstead than I ever had before – Georgian, Victorian, Edwardian, all there, muddled up together and yet somehow fitting. This, I thought, is where I want to have a house, as near to the Heath as possible.

I spent six weeks at home in Heath Villas, writing a novel and then, when an agent I sent it to turned it down (though what his reply actually said was 'come and see me' and I interpreted that as a rejection), I began teaching. I didn't want to be a teacher but it was the only job I thought I was qualified to do. (In 1960, it was reckoned that a degree was enough, with no extra training.) I left the house every weekday to get two buses to Paddington where I'd been sent as a supply teacher to a secondary modern school there. The job was quite well paid and all my earnings were going towards buying a house one day, so however hard the work it was worth it with such an end in the far distance. On the bus, I read a newspaper which at that time had a double-page spread summarising current affairs for easy under-standing. I absorbed the main points and then, whatever lesson I was supposed to be teaching, I taught current affairs instead. The children quite liked this, preferring it to maths or geography or any other lesson, and the other teachers didn't care so long as they themselves didn't have to fill in for the absent real teacher. I went from Paddington to various other schools, a week at a time usually, and then I was sent to Barnsbury, in Islington, for a whole term.

This school was still a secondary modern, but it was much better than any of the others I'd been allocated to. There was no getting away with cobbled-together current affairs lessons, for a start. I was filling in for an English teacher on maternity leave and I was expected to carry on with the syllabus she'd been teaching. I settled in quickly, and though it was exhausting it could also be rewarding. Half the battle, as every teacher knows, was imposing discipline, which to me was simply a form of acting – acting harsh, acting fierce, acting stern. I'd cast myself in different parts according to the behaviour of the class and once I'd got control of the more rowdy elements I had no trouble with the actual teaching.

It was always, during this period at Barnsbury (which went on two years in all, with a proper job offered after that first term) such a comfort coming back to Heath Villas. I had such an easy and pleasant journey to and from school every day, walking as I did across the edge of the Heath to the South End Green overground station where I took a train a few stops to Barnsbury, then had a short walk to the school itself. However tired I was at the end of each school day, the climb up the hill into the Vale of Health was always soothing. I always came the back way, cutting across Lime Avenue to approach the pond and stood watching the ducks and the occasional swan before going round the corner to Heath Villas. Twentieth-century life fell away, and I always felt that at any minute one of the literary luminaries who had lived in the Vale might suddenly appear to admire the view I was admiring. Entering our house, the intense silence added to this feeling that this could not be London, that I could not be living so near to its centre.

But I was, we were. The strange thing was that we were not tucked away in some backwater with little idea of what was going on in the wider London world outside our house. On the contrary, we were part of it, leading a very London life in spite of where we lived. Hunter was now on the *Sunday Times* and all kinds of perks came with the job. We went to theatres' first nights, openings of new films, previews at art galleries and to every kind of restaurant. Coming back to the Vale of Health after these evenings it seemed more and more incredible that it could exist, so free of noise and traffic, untouched by the feverish atmosphere of the West End. The only time there was any disturbance was on bank holidays when the fair arrived. Then, the road into the Vale would get jammed, and crowds would spill out all round it coming to enjoy the roundabouts and other fairground attractions. Even so, the sounds that floated above the tree tops were not deafening by the time they reached our windows, but instead simply lively and somehow quaint, a reminder of all the other times the fair had come over the years, giving a reassuring feeling of continuity. Even Mr Elton didn't object to this particular, short-lived racket, and Mrs Woodcock never referred to it as vulgar.

Once, around the time of a fair, Mr Elton took us out for the evening, an obvious sign that he approved of us as tenants. He took us to a variety show at the Victoria Palace theatre, and then for dinner at Overton's the fish restaurant. It emerged afterwards that he'd gone to see the show first, to be sure that it was enjoyable, because he didn't want to risk disappointing us. The highlight, in his opinion, was a man who imitated bird songs – 'extraordinary, as if there were a blackbird in the theatre' – and a juggling act – 'marvellous dexterity'. He hardly ate any of his dinner, but we scoffed ours, appreciating the food and wine rather more than the bird noises. Over the meal, he made it clear that he was very happy to have us in his house and that he felt we fitted in remarkably well. We were pleased with the compliment, knowing it was a genuine mark of favour bestowed upon us because Mr Elton loved his house and wanted to see it loved by others. We got on so well with him but he was still shy and went on communicating by hand-written note. These notes were left on the hall table, where Mrs Woodcock also left hers, and we replied to them the same way. Sometimes it became quite ridiculous, with us passing each other on the stairs to leave a note saying what could easily be said in person, but still I loved this form of communication. It suited the house. Telephones, though of course we used them, didn't. The moment ours started to ring, I'd leap to silence it. Notes were quiet. They gave time to think and compose a reply at leisure. If Mr Elton was eccentric using them, then I was just as eccentric myself, encouraging him. The house, I felt, approved.

After almost three years of living at Heath Villas the time to leave was coming. We didn't want to, and Mr Elton didn't want us to, but we wanted to own a house and stop paying rent (six guineas a week). We also were beginning to realise we wanted children. So, in the autumn of 1962, we began looking for a house in Hampstead. What a joke! Our limit was £5,000 (with a substantial mortgage to obtain, of course). There was no house in Hampstead proper for that price.

At first, we refused to believe what the estate agents told us, diligently searching every road and square, convinced there must be some little house everyone else had overlooked, or had thought too dilapidated to take on. We would find it. But after weeks of tramping round, we began to give up hope. Facts had to be faced, and the facts were that we couldn't afford a house in Hampstead and if we were still stuck on buying a house then we would have to forget Hampstead and move away. Either that or we could perhaps buy a flat – in one of the big mansions in areas like Frognal. We'd lived happily in our current flat and could very likely find an equally good but roomier flat where children were not forbidden.

No. No because we longed for the independence and privacy a house would bring. So we began looking round the fringes of South End Green where there were some houses, in poor condition, just over our limit, which might be possible, but they were invariably under offer before we even got to look round them. Next stop was Kentish Town. I hated Kentish Town High Road, a long, flat traffic-choked road with scruffy shops either side. The estate agent there was Jennings & Sampson, who had on their books houses in the streets leading off this depressing High Road for which we might be able to get a mortgage. I wouldn't go inside some of them. Just standing there, so near the thunder and dirt of the main road, I thought how depressed I'd get coming home to this every day. Having a house wouldn't be worth it. The situation mattered, maybe not as much as the house itself but still, it mattered. A house for sale in Tufnell Park, out of the range of the High Road, sounded better. It would be a brisk, fifteen-minute walk to the Heath, but for a fit couple in their mid-twenties that was nothing. This house, though, had five storeys, and if we bought it we'd have to let half of it, and we didn't want to become landlords ourselves.

On and on it went, this trailing round looking at houses we didn't like, in roads where we didn't want to live, and every time coming back to the idyllic Vale of Health. We'd been round and round the Heath several times, searching all the fringes. Page 44 of the A–Z was tattered with use and increasingly we were thumbing page 45. Then, in late November, wearily looking yet again at what Jennings & Sampson had on offer, we saw another house for sale. It was in Parliament Hill Fields, on page 45, the other side of Highgate Road. It was described as flat-fronted, semi-detached, with a pleasant garden. There was a drawback, which was that the house had a sitting tenant, paying one pound and twelve shillings a week, living on the top floor. Sitting tenants were protected by law and there was little hope of getting them to leave unless there was an impressive financial inducement, which we wouldn't be in a position to offer. The house itself was probably in need of modernising – 'ideally suited for the discriminate buyer who is desirous of carrying out repairs and redecorations to his own requirements' was clear estate-agent language for 'it's a wreck'. But it was near the Heath, very near, if on what was then thought the wrong side, so we went to look at it, on a bitterly cold, snowy day.

The approach was promising. Coming from the Vale of Health, we saw, as we crossed Highgate Road, a fine Georgian terrace set back from the road, with trees and some grass in front of it. The house we'd come to view was in Boscastle Road, directly behind this terrace. We crossed Highgate Road into Dartmouth Park Road, a wide street with four-storey houses either side, and then left into Boscastle Road itself, another generously broad road. We were early for our appointment with the estate agent and had plenty of time to stand and stare at the house. It had a reassuringly solid look about it. The large floor-to-ceiling windows on the first floor looked like those of our flat in Heath Villas. That was good. So was the broad windowsill on the ground floor – I immediately imagined boxes there, full of geraniums cascading down the front, mixed in with some trailing ivy. How pretty it would look, especially with fresh paint everywhere and a bright yellow front door.

The estate agent, when he arrived, had a struggle opening the front door. He blamed the snow, claiming there was nothing wrong with the lock it was just jammed up with icy particles. Eventually, after he'd twisted and turned the key several more times, the door began to yield. He still had to give it a hard push, but it creaked open enough to allow us to enter. We shuffled into the hall, and then recoiled from the smell. Even the estate agent suddenly had trouble breathing as he muttered that the house had been shut up a long time, which accounted, he maintained, for 'the lack of fresh air'. But he knew, and we knew, the smell, the stench was due to more than the house having been closed up. It was the smell of decay somewhere, dead rats maybe, or of blocked drains, or of rubbish piled up in some forgotten corner. Whatever the source, it was an overpoweringly evil smell.

We stood in the gloomy hall, looking at the dark brown embossed wallpaper covering the lower part of the walls. Above the dado rail which ran along the top there was dull beige wallpaper, some of it peeling off the wall revealing crumbling plaster. There was a little light leaking in from the glass pane above the front door, but this wasn't enough to see anything properly, which was maybe just as well. The estate agent moved us quickly into the front room, which had heavy wooden shutters, meaning there was even less light here than there had been in the hall. He opened them with a flourish, and one immediately came off its hinges. Undeterred, he drew our attention to the 'fine genuine marble fireplace' and commented on the 'generous proportions of the room'. We shifted uneasily on the bare floorboards, aware that some of them were clearly splintered and would maybe give way. The estate agent pointed to the ceiling rose and said it was 'genuine'. We gazed upwards, but more at the bare wire hanging down than at the plaster decoration. But we were being moved on rapidly to the back room, dark not because of any closed shutters but because the light from the window was blocked by the back additions to the house. There must have only been a couple of hours a day when the sun could shine directly in, such was the tunnel effect. One of these additions was the kitchen. The estate agent was silenced, knowing nothing could be said to put any kind of gloss on the state this room was in. It looked as if no attempt had been made to clean it for years. The sink was black with dirt, half-full of scummy water which had lumps of grey matter, impossible to identify, floating in it. There was an ancient cooker, the top an inch deep in filth, with the door hanging off. A board running from cooker to sink was covered in a red and white patterned plastic, greasy and slimy. 'The kitchen needs modernising, obviously,' the estate agent said. Obviously.

Upstairs was less depressing. The front first-floor sitting room lifted our spirits. Even on that sunless day, it was full of light from the two big windows we'd admired from outside. Here, too, there was a marble fireplace, but this one was clean and, surprisingly, a fire was laid in it, looking so neat, ready to have a match put to it. There was no furniture, but there was a carpet, plain fawn with a darker brown rim, and though it had some stains on it, it gave the room a lived-in feeling the rest of the house lacked. The bedroom, the back room on the first floor, was in reasonable condition too, painted not wallpapered, and the view from the window was an overview of the whole garden, not visible from the room below. We peered out at the trees and bushes shrouded in snow, and tried to guess what they were. Apple trees, plum, cherry? Lilac bushes, camellias, forsythia? Who knew – certainly not the estate agent. Consulting his notes, he pronounced the garden 'well stocked'.

This left the bathroom, and the top floor rented by the sitting tenant. The bathroom was, as expected, 'in need of modernisation'. The bath itself was a rather handsome tub, though badly stained. The lavatory was separate. The lid was down, and nobody, least of all the estate agent, was bold enough to lift it or to pull the metal chain. The top floor was another two sets of stairs up and the smell here was different, certainly not as foul but cloying in a different way. We stood and looked into each of the three rooms, all of them crowded with furniture, and the windows both net-curtained and with heavy brocade curtains, almost closed, over them. The sitting tenant was in America, visiting her daughter. She'd been there six months and, though this was not actually said, the impression was given that she might not return.

That was it. We went back to the Vale of Health confused and dispirited. The house was in a much worse condition than we'd anticipated and it was obvious a great deal of 'modernisation' would have to be done, at a huge cost. We didn't have the money to finance all the essential work. But more serious than this worry was the question, did we really want this house? Does it speak to us, we asked each other mockingly. No. The answer was a resounding No. On the contrary, it yelled at us to run a mile. Its voice, if it had had one, couldn't compete with that of Heath Villas. It was like looking at someone clad in filthy, tattered garments, their unwashed grey hair lying lank around their scab-covered face, and trying to see what might lie underneath this woeful appearance after a good scrubbing. Was there a sound, even attractive, body under this outer grime? Maybe there was, but had we the nerve, never mind the money, to bet on it? Would we be able to tolerate a sitting tenant? Would we get on with her as well as we had done with Mr Elton and Mrs Woodcock?

The agonising went on and on: to make a bid, or not? In the end, we made an offer of £5,000, just below the asking price. I didn't know if I wanted it to be accepted or not. Yes, I wanted to have a house, I'd always wanted this, but not in any old condition. When our offer was accepted, I didn't know whether to be thrilled, or to be alarmed. There was no jump-for-joy while we waited to see if we could get the necessary mortgage – which we did. The Scottish Union said they would give us £3,600 on a twenty-year mortgage, if first of all the roof was mended together with some other less vital conditions. Our savings covered the rest of the cost, leaving us with a mere few hundred to pay for the building work (or at least to begin to pay for it while we earned more).

The agreement was signed on 18th February 1963. It felt terrifying. We picked up the keys and went into the house, our house. It still smelled bad, it was still unwelcoming, sulking, not at all pleased to see us. We wandered about all the rooms, making lists of what needed to be done.

There was no feeling of elation whatsoever.

BOSCASTLE ROAD

N.W.5
London

Leaving our flat in Heath Villas was hard. It felt so sad, looking round the first floor for the last time, a weak, wintry sun creeping across the carpet, lighting the whole place up as it always did. The house we were going to was dark in comparison, with no views from most of its windows except for rows of other houses. Here, we'd looked out on greenery everywhere, and the still waters of the pond. These two rooms, the sitting room and the kitchen, had lifted the spirits, always. And they had been lucky for us. Everything went right, the three years we lived there, and I thought it was not too fanciful to imagine that the atmosphere here, and of the house itself, had helped. This house had been a turning point. It's where I wrote and had accepted by Jonathan Cape the book that would become my first novel, and now I could begin to make at least some sort of living as a writer.

But however much we loved it, we were leaving. Mrs Woodcock gave me a leaving present: a silver Queen Anne mirror, a rather odd gift but very kind of her. She said she would miss us and wished we were 'not going so far away' (though of course we were hardly going any distance at all). Mr Elton took us out to a farewell meal and then gave us two large china breakfast cups and saucers decorated in a pattern of pale green leaves. He wasn't actually in the house when we left – he said he found goodbyes distressing – but Mrs Woodcock stood at her window and as the van we'd hired drove off she waved a white handkerchief. Oh, dear me, it would have taken a heart of stone indeed not to weep, which I proceeded to do, bawling all the short way to Boscastle Road. The only way I could make myself stop snivelling was by telling myself that we were only leaving the Vale of Health for a few years. We would be back, or back in Hampstead anyway, when we'd made some money. Boscastle Road was only to be temporary, our first house, to be followed by what would be our *real* house. This wreck we were moving to, which would drain our slim purse and our energy, was a mere stepping stone, okay? OK.

Snow was still lingering on the ground. The cold was bitter that March day. We had the same trouble opening the front door as the estate agent had had, even though we'd been in and out several times since. It seemed a bad omen to have to struggle to get into what was now our house, and I began to imagine it had some dreadful history we didn't yet know about. But, so far as available records could reveal, it didn't. Its history was quite ordinary. The land the house was built on had been leased first to one William Apedaile of New Hampton, Middlesex, and then to John Edgar, a builder living in Kentish Town. Previously, the land belonged to the Earl of Dartmouth, which is why several roads in the area were given his name. John Edgar built his first eight houses in 1869, and then sold one to Margaret Jane Hollick, who in turn sold it in 1929 to Victor Prior, a musician. The next owners were the Ligate family. James Ligate was an engine driver, and he lived in our house with his two sisters Ellen and May. Ellen was the last to die. She took in lodgers, and the last of them was Mrs Hall who moved in just before the Rent Act of 1957. She occupied the top floor, but after Ellen

Ligate's death the rest of the house remained empty, while its ownership was disputed, though there were some short-term lettings.

Nothing there to account for the sullen feel to this house. For such a long time, it seemed to resist all efforts to make it a pleasant place to come home to. It sulked and scowled and seemed determined to stick to its unlovely state however hard we tried to clean and modernise it. We camped in one room, the bedroom, where at least the view of the garden cheered us up – ah, the garden, upon which the Ligates had lavished all the attention lacking in the house. It was one of the unexpected consolations of those first weeks in the house, watching the shape of the garden emerge as spring arrived. Every day we saw some new treasure, one day a tree revealed, in its froth of white blossom, as an apple tree, another a shrub as a japonica or forsythia or lilac . . . colour, colour everywhere and faint scents wafting through the windows, now wide open to try to lift the still lingering mouldy smell. Later on, there were roses emerging, with an arch entwined with them halfway down the path, and either side of this path there were flowers we were too ignorant to give a name to. The whole of this pampered garden was walled, an old brick wall, and at the end there was an Anderson air-raid shelter. There was space to build a garage, opening onto the mews lane between us and Grove Terrace, if we so wished. We did wish, but a garage was well down the list of essential jobs.

The surveyor's instructions had been clear: the roof was the main priority. The valley gutters needed renewing and the tiles of the whole roof would have to be overhauled. Obviously, we needed a builder. Mr Elton recommended the Hampstead firm of Cramb and Dean. Someone came to give an estimate, but it was three times that of the local Kentish Town builder we found. We knew this might mean the local man, one J.P. Brown, was rubbish but we took the chance, and he and his merry men got cracking. J.P. Brown was an Irishman, thickset and strong looking though not young. There was nothing about his appearance which inspired confidence except for his brawny arms, the sleeves of his shirt always rolled up, ready for work and looking used to it. He was cheerful and full of confidence – the roof would be no bother, no bother at all. He had a gang of six Irish workmen who all lived in his house in Fortess Road, ten minutes away. They seemed to sleep in a kind of dormitory, so far as our questioning could make out, with Mrs Brown cooking their dinner every evening, the money to pay for it taken out of their wages before they got them. They arrived promptly at 7.30 each morning, though not always all six, and took possession of the house before we left for work (I was still teaching). They could tell how worried we were, especially me, about all the work that needed to be done but it only seemed to amuse them. 'Will ye look at that?' they'd say, pointing out some dodgy brickwork, 'falling down, 'tis!' and then merely laugh, and tell me they were only joking – 'It'll be a grand house when we've done, so it will,' they'd console me. I found it hard to believe. For weeks and weeks, all was destruction, the tearing out of things leaving gaping holes which terrified me. The noise was coming from so many different places, the hammering and drilling and sawing, and the bad smell was replaced by other hardly less unpleasant odours of cement and plaster and thick dust. If there was a plan, any order in this chaos, then it was all in J.P. Brown's head.

He himself often wasn't there, and sometimes none of his men were either. They just disappeared, with no warning. There was never any explanation afterwards either, though clearly they were moving between jobs. We'd phone J.P. Brown, and get Mrs Brown, who always sounded breathless, as though she'd climbed a great number of stairs to answer the phone, which had rung long enough to force her to answer. She never had the least idea where either her husband or his crew were. 'Out, working,' she would say. Sometimes she was too exhausted, or too fed-up to speak, and would simply lift the receiver and wait. When we asked for J.P. she'd say, ''tis Mrs Brown' and hang up. Eventually, we discovered that if she was pestered enough she'd nag her husband to come to us, because we'd become, with our anxious pleading, 'that poor young couple'. This, so the workmen told us, hugely enjoying the drama, infuriated their boss, who would shout at her in the name of Jesus to shut up. But it usually resulted in him sending at least a couple of the workmen round the next day.

Sometimes, he'd send one of his sons to oversee. The workmen liked this. It meant Brown junior arriving at 7.30 a.m. and leaving at 8 a.m. to have breakfast. He was a carpenter, but they had absolute contempt for him, a contempt shared by his father. The son put cupboards in with such carelessness that none of the joins fitted. 'Call himself a chippy,' his father would mutter, and kick the cupboard door to demonstrate how badly it was hung. When J.P. himself was there, twice as much work was done, as he rushed backwards and forwards through the house inspecting and examining everything and blaspheming loudly if it was not to his satisfaction. He went on the roof himself, doing most of the retiling, completely oblivious to any wind blowing, holding on his battered old cap, however unsteady it made him. Standing in the garden watching him was a terrifying experience (and many years later, we heard that was how J.P. Brown died, swept off a roof in a strong wind he'd chosen to ignore).

We were still, after three months, living in one room, our bedroom (though we had a cooker functioning in the still hellhole of a kitchen). We'd allowed ourselves the luxury of a fitted carpet there, a cheap hair cord, pale green and very Heath Villas. We were only in this room to sleep because as soon as we came home from work we would start trying to tackle all the jobs that needed to be done. J.P. Brown was being paid to do the building work, but we couldn't afford to pay him to do the decorating. This, we assured each other, we could do ourselves. It was just a case, wasn't it, of stripping off old wallpaper and paint, and putting new stuff on? Any fool could do that. It turned out, of course, that it was harder than it looked and that we were hopeless at this DIY. We couldn't make the dark brown embossed paper on the hall walls budge. First we attacked it with metal scrapers, then with some sort of liquid which had acid in it – 'will remove even the most stubborn wallpaper' – and still it clung on. It was the same with the thick brown paint on the doors which we daringly tried to remove with a blowlamp. Hours and hours we spent on these sorts of jobs, getting more and more bad-tempered and tired.

The house itself seemed to be resisting all our valiant efforts to make it look good. It was as though it had no intention of yielding to the 1960s, with its liking for white paint and plain surfaces, and wanted instead to cling on to dreary colours and florid wallpapers, stuck in the Victorian era. This resistance was particularly evident when it came to the floors. Bare, sealed floorboards were the thing in 1963. We'd seen them in other houses and we wanted them in ours. Knowing it would be a task probably beyond us, we asked J.P. Brown to do it when he'd finished the building work. He said no, it would be robbing us. The floorboards were in poor condition, and were only cheap wood anyway, and they would split if they were sanded. He demonstrated by helpfully putting the heel of his boot through one floorboard which already had a crack in it. Couldn't he replace just the boards which had splits in them? No, he couldn't, there were too many of them. Best to put a nice bit of lino down. We sulked, then we turned stubborn and hired a sanding machine. We were terrified of it, but off we went, sanding the boards of the ground floor, holding our breath in case every single one splintered. Not quite half of them did, but we splashed on the seal and pretended it had worked. We could almost hear the house sniggering at the result, and we certainly heard J.P. laughing when he next turned up. He was kind, though, directing one of his men to put nails here and there in the places where boards were coming adrift.

Meanwhile, the main work had all been done. The back addition was now a proper kitchen with a new window overlooking the garden. The bathroom had a new bath, sink and lavatory. We had had central heating installed, though we hadn't yet used it. The horrible smell had gone. Now, coming into the house, the smell was of paint. One job we found we could manage satisfactorily was painting the walls – any fool really could do that. We bought two sheepskin rollers ('don't be bothering with the foam ones,' J.P. said), price: £1.8s.6d, and set to. Every wall was now white, pristine and perfect. We even accomplished the harder task of laying a tiled floor in the kitchen, black and white tiles, to achieve what we hoped would be a Dutch interior effect. The house, at last, was agreeing to scrub up well.

It was at this point, just as we felt we were truly taking possession of our house, that our sitting tenant arrived back from America. We soon discovered we had been deluded.

The moment Mrs Hall arrived back we felt we were living once more in a flat, a large and roomy flat, but a flat all the same. Up to then, it had been easy to forget that the top floor of our house was lived in by someone else, who would have habits, routines, tastes which did not fit with ours. Sharing a house with Mrs Hall turned out to be not at all like sharing with Mrs Woodcock and Mr Elton. Mrs Hall did not flit silently up and down the shared staircase as Mr Elton had done. For a woman in her mid-sixties – a small, slight woman – she was surprisingly heavy on her feet, thumping up and down the stairs as though she were wearing hobnailed boots instead of perfectly ordinary shoes. She clearly liked her passage through the house to be noted, pausing often to sigh or groan in a highly theatrical way. It brought me out of whatever room I was in to enquire if she was all right, and gave her the opportunity to describe her various ailments, and me to show some sympathy. She liked to talk, and had absolutely no intention of communicating by note. I tried that once only, leaving a polite note at the bottom of her stairs, the extra two flights that went up to her floor, telling her that one of the workmen would be coming up to mend the leaking tap she'd reported. She came down to the kitchen holding it at arm's length, rather the way Mrs Woodcock held the *Sunday Times* colour magazine when she was disposing of it, and said, 'What's this? Am I not worth talking to now?' I apologised, said I just thought it easier to leave a note, it meant there was no need to bother her. 'Bother?' she said, 'Talking to me is a bother?' I gave up, and never left a note again.

We shared a bathroom and lavatory with Mrs Hall, just as we had done with Mr Elton. Every morning at 6 a.m. Mrs Hall thundered down her stairs to use the lavatory, and after she'd used it she sprayed an air-freshener vigorously, repeated puffs of some stuff supposed to smell like roses according to the label, and in fact stinking of decaying vegetation. We asked her if she would please just open the window instead because we didn't like the smell of the spray. She said would we prefer lily of the valley, or Devon violets, the spray came in those scents too. No, we said, sorry, but just open the window, fresh air is best. Not, she said, at her age, opening a window at that time would likely bring on her cough. So we had to put up with it, and open the window ourselves when we got up.

Even more annoying were the rubber stickers she stuck on the bottom of our new bath. These were blue, shaped like stars, and were to make the bath safe for her. They'd been bought in America and she expected us to be thrilled with them, saying they would prevent us from having accidents ourselves. I tried to get them off, but couldn't. They remained there, irritating me every single day, for the next fifteen years, until we got a new bath.

Air fresheners and star stickers caused nothing like the fury the arrival of Mrs Hall's television caused. Her daughter in America bought it for her, and she was very proud of having it. In 1963, televisions were not at all common – we didn't have one ourselves – and she invited her friends to come and watch in the evenings. We then had a procession of excited elderly women hauling themselves up the stairs, with Mrs Hall instructing them to 'hang on to the banisters,' as though the staircase itself was in danger of moving. They then settled down to watch this modern marvel, with the sound turned up to top volume. Mrs Hall had told us she was 'hard of hearing' but she had no faith in hearing aids and wouldn't succumb to them. She was fond of musical programmes and any sort of quiz or game show, and we'd hear these booming away, the astonishingly loud noise percolating through the entire house. The friends all left by nine o'clock usually, but the television stayed on until midnight when Mrs Hall finally went to bed. It was directly over our bedroom and we'd lie there fuming, thinking this can't go on, it's ridiculous, this is *our* house and she's dominating it. We wondered if we could get J.P. to put a wall and a door at the bottom of Mrs Hall's stairs, to cut out the noise, but knew it wouldn't work, and then we thought of moving our bedroom downstairs but we didn't want to and why the hell should we. The only other option was to buy her out, but we didn't have the money. She was rightly protected by the Rent Act of 1957, which gave her the right to stay so long as she paid the rent, and we had always known this. We'd recently been told we were allowed to increase her rent of one pound twelve shillings a week to two guineas and rather hoped she would say this was too much and she was going to find somewhere cheaper. No chance. She paid her rent scrupulously every week, in cash, counting it out coin by coin in front of us, to emphasise her unquestionable honesty. No one enjoyed being a sitting tenant more than Mrs Hall. She was well aware of her power in the house: we needn't think it was ours. She'd been here first, and her hold on it was firm.

So for five years, from 1963–68, we learned to tolerate Mrs Hall. This would have been easier if she hadn't had such a strong personality, and if she hadn't been such a complainer. She complained about things you would have thought she'd be glad of, such as the central heating. Before we came, her flat was heated by two electric fires which were an expensive form of heating and didn't, I imagine, warm her whole flat very effectively. It seemed sensible when J.P. Brown was putting central heating in the rest of the house also to have it extended to the top floor which, of course, one day we hoped to have access to. But Mrs Hall was not pleased. She complained that there were not enough radiators provided and the heat was inadequate. There was no possibility of comparing and contrasting the heat now with the heat of the previous electric fires, so we had to take her word for it even though we doubted she was right. She also thought she was entitled to have all three of her rooms redecorated because marks had been made on her paintwork during the installation of the central heating.

Sometimes, she went away, though not yet for another visit to America (for which we yearned). That wasn't due for another three years, 'if I'm spared'. But she occasionally went to stay for a weekend with her other daughter who lived half an hour away and came to collect her by car. Then, the house returned to us, though these brief respites made us even more eager to have it to ourselves all the time. There was one way, though, in which having Mrs Hall there proved an asset.

In March 1964, I had my first baby, Caitlin, and instantly Mrs Hall changed character. The television was no longer blaring away until midnight for fear it might waken the baby, and she began tiptoeing up and down the stairs, shushing her friends too. By the time Caitlin was fifteen months and able to crawl up stairs, Mrs Hall tempted her up to her flat every day. This was excellent news for me. I didn't actively encourage Caitlin to climb Mrs Hall's stairs but I didn't stop her, especially once I was pregnant again and welcomed the rest I could have while she was with Mrs Hall.

I was going to give birth this time at home, and we were having the coalhouse converted into a small bedroom. We once more had J.P. Brown back. It wasn't a big job, only a matter of clearing this back addition of remnants of coal and other rubbish, putting a window in, and then knocking a door through into the main house. By then, the house had changed its nature convincingly and this was just another improvement. I'd first realised this transformation when I came home from hospital with Caitlin and saw the house in a completely different light. I came back to it, my mind still half expecting it to seem not really ours. I was like a stranger, seeing it all anew, and I could hardly believe how light and bright and attractive it was. It was a snowy day, just as it had been when we first saw the house, but this time the yellow painted door with its shining brass knocker opened smoothly, and inside the walls were papered in a blue and white pattern of birds, and the sitting room had a log fire burning and it was all clean and lovely.

Jake was born in May 1966, in the new, little room, probably the first baby ever to be born in the house. I loved this fact. People had died in the house but nobody had been born there so far as we could find out, and this made it belong even more to us. Unable to resist a sentimental gesture to mark the occasion, we planted a cherry tree in the garden. There were plenty of fruit trees in it already, but none planted by us, so this one was special (and it went on to flourish, cascading the lawn with pink blossom every spring). It made me begin to decide that we could never leave this house, our house. How could we, when we'd planted a tree and needed to watch it mature? Would returning to Hampstead be worth such desertion? No, it would not. Already, in a mere three years the 'significant moments' had piled up and were exerting a powerful tug on my loyalty to the house. But it wasn't a decision that needed to be made yet, because we were nowhere near being able to move back to the Vale of Health, or anywhere similar. The thought was there, though, at the back of my mind: I am not going to want to leave this house, ever.

But if Heath Villas had brought us luck there were signs, by 1966, that Boscastle Road was going to be even luckier for us. The next two years were hectic, with film projects on the go which made it look as if we were at last going to refill our bank account, emptied by paying for all the work done by J.P. Brown. My second novel, *Georgy Girl*, was in production, and Hunter's *Here We Go Round the Mulberry Bush* was on the edge of the same. Our house, during this period, became a place of meetings – directors, producers and actors – which I didn't like at all. I felt uncomfortable having these people in my house, though they were being very accommodating and kind, agreeing to come to me, first because I was about to have Jake and then after I'd had him. It wasn't, for them, a very workman-like atmosphere, sitting in a room full of toys and baby clothes, with one child tottering around and the other roaring in his cradle only just next door and not at all out of hearing. They were tolerant, these men, sitting with scripts on their knees, pointing out what would work and what would not, and I was the impatient one, knowing I wasn't suited for this or for any kind of team work.

Mrs Hall, on the other hand, loved all this activity. The film people came in large cars, which often waited in the street for them. Though she said she was 'hard of hearing', she somehow seemed to hear our doorbell ring before I did and would rush down, arthritic limbs suddenly nimble, and answer the door, claiming she'd thought it was *her* bell being rung. We also, around this time, had some television crews arriving to do interviews which changed Mrs Hall's attitude to us entirely. She was disappointed when told that the programmes we'd appear on were obscure arts slots which she'd be unlikely to catch. But still, we had had television made *in our house* – the glory of it. I was relieved that by the time Hunter was doing the Beatles' biography, and they themselves were coming to the house, Mrs Hall was in America again for another six months. Answering the door to the Fab Four would have had her swooning.

Why exactly the Beatles wanted to come to our house never seemed clear to me. What was the attraction? I thought maybe it was a kind of joke even if I didn't understand it. But Hunter insisted it was part of wanting, at the height of their fame and already tired of it, to do 'normal' things. Going to friends' houses for dinner was what 'normal' people did in the new middle-class life they, like us, had fallen into. Anyway, three of them came, separately, though I'd rather have got the whole thing over in one go.

Paul came first, with Jane Asher, but for tea, not dinner. Tea was easy. Paul played energetically with Jake, and Jane charmed Caitlin. Next came George and Pattie, but for an evening meal. George was intent on a philo-sophical discussion, and not much interested in the food. I'd been told all the Beatles were vegetarians (not at all common in the sixties) and I'd gone to some trouble to prepare an aubergine dish from a recipe I'd learned. I made the same dish for Ringo and Maureen but it turned out they were the sort of vegetarians who didn't like vegetables other than potatoes. Luckily, I'd made two puddings, so that was fine. John, in the end, didn't come, having got over any desire to do the middle-class thing (and anyway, unlike the other three, all brought up, like us, in council houses, John was nearer to being middle class himself).

It was as a direct result of earnings from films and the Beatles' biography, on which we had already paid tax, that we, too, were about to leave our house and go abroad for fourteen months. I was appalled at the idea. We'd just got the house into shape and had actually been able to furnish it – why would I want to leave my brand-new

Habitat day-bed and the big pine table and the squishy, low armchairs? I was still at the point of admiring them all (Mrs Woodcock's influence long since rejected). I was settled and didn't want to be uprooted, and most of all I did not want other people renting our house, which is what would have to happen if we went off for this allegedly idyllic year or so in the Mediterranean. But it was explained to me that, with tax under Harold Wilson's Labour government now at around ninety-five per cent, if we didn't go abroad we would lose the rest of this sudden influx of money. We might never earn such sums again, and by keeping a proportion of it, if we went abroad, we would give ourselves security for the future. The other factors that came into the decision were that Hunter had been given a sabbatical year by the *Sunday Times*, and both children were not yet school age. It was the perfect opportunity to spend it in a *Swiss Family Robinson* kind of way.

I still wasn't jumping for joy.

A New Zealand family rented our house for a year. They were enthusiastic about the house, thrilled with the garden, and delighted to be so near Hampstead Heath. Their two children were the same age as Caitlin and Jake, and slotted perfectly into the playroom (the name given by then to any room where children slept and had their toys, the word 'nursery', now outdated). I wanted to ask them to cherish all our belongings but couldn't, knowing it would be a cheek when they were paying to use them – 'cherish' indeed! They asked if they could move in some of their own bits and pieces, which they'd bought while in an unfurnished flat for the last three months, and we said of course. There turned out to be quite a lot of these 'bits and pieces' and once they'd arrived they fitted in oddly with our own furniture. Rooms which had had plenty of space in them suddenly looked crowded. They also asked if they could move some furniture of ours to other rooms, in an arrangement that would suit them better, and again we said yes, of course they could do whatever they wanted once we had left, but could they put everything back as it had been before they, in turn, departed.

Fuss, fuss . . . it was only furniture, and I could put everything back as it had been in half an hour, so it was ridiculous to mind so much about the position of objects. But already, with the New Zealanders' stuff in place before we left, the house felt as if it had passed out of my hands. The red, wooden rocking chair, my latest purchase, looked all wrong now that it had been moved from the corner near the window to accommodate the new family's giant trunk, and our big pine table was wasted, shoved up against a wall so that their two-seater sofa could fit in. Our Welsh dresser – another, now fashionable item – was festooned with the New Zealanders' new crockery instead of my arty display of old china plates, and the kitchen had gained a pressure cooker, an ugly, shiny chrome thing. Definitely time to go.

I hated closing the front door behind us as we left, early one raw March morning, a taxi taking us to Heathrow. I was pushing emotion onto what was just a pile of bricks and mortar, a place I'd only lived in for five years, imagining that the house was giving a forlorn cry of abandonment as the key was turned in the lock. All the other houses I'd lived in, except for our rented flat in Heath Villas, I'd left without a backward look, and now here I was, 'carrying on' as my father would have said, and yet I was only leaving this particular house for fourteen months. What had happened? I really didn't know, but there was already an attachment there that took me by surprise.

An Interlude:
BIRBUDA STREET

Gozo
Quinta das Redes
Algarve

The house we arrived at, in the Maltese island of Gozo, was not the house we'd thought we would be living in. That one, which we'd been shown slides of, was above Ramla beach, the only good sandy beach on the island. It had looked idyllic, situated on a hill just above the beach, with a narrow path running down to it. But at the last minute, literally the day before we left England, we were told that this house was no longer available but there was another, even better, in the north of the island. We had no alternative but to accept it.

It was not 'better' than the Ramla beach one. For a start, it was nowhere near a beach, any beach. The address, Birbuda Street, Ghaab, suggested some kind of organised community but the reality was a dispersed collection of houses stuck at the far north of the island, not exactly a wilderness but tending that way. The last bit of the road to it was stony and dusty and we were relieved to get to the end. The house itself, when we found it, at least looked attractively Moorish in design. It had recently been converted from an abandoned farmhouse and nobody had yet lived in it in its new form. I'd worried about fitting in to somebody else's house, but there was no difficulty there. The house had no atmosphere about it at all. It felt blank, without any imprint of any kind. Entering it was like stepping into a vault, with the ceiling so high and the walls whitewashed and bare. It felt cool, which was a blessing after the blazing heat outdoors, and there was a faint echo when we talked. It was quite dark, the main light coming from the door, which opened onto a long veranda.

We unpacked our luggage, our clothes, toys and books, and they immediately looked lost. The furniture was basic and cheap, not at all suited to its setting. A Formica table with spindly legs looked like an insult to the living room as did two armchairs covered in grey moquette. At least, we thought, the children can't damage anything, and there was the advantage of having lots of space for them to run around in. But from the beginning, there was no sense either that this house had ever been someone's home or that it could be made into one, and certainly not during the short time we were going to be there. It was a house made to be rented, to provide an income for its new, absent, owners, and that was how it would remain.

It proved a strange experience living there. Two maids went with the house, twins called Josephine and Lily, who spoke little English. We weren't given any choice about having them – they were part of the deal, and turned up every morning for two hours, though there was little to do. A great deal of sweeping went on, and a lot of clothes washing (there was, of course, no washing machine). They were always snatching up clothes that didn't need to be washed, and then scrubbing them ferociously, over and over again, in a big tub. We usually left for the beach soon after they arrived, and returned as they were leaving, so we didn't get in each other's way. We had a long siesta in the afternoon and then, when it was cooler, though not much cooler, we would go and explore the rest of the island. At night, the house was hot, though it felt cool during the day, and we slept badly. It was a relief when dawn came, the coolest part of the day.

We knew, quite early on, that we'd made a mistake and part of this mistake was the house itself, not just its situation, though this was a disaster. It seemed a long car ride from Ramla beach, where we'd wanted to be and where we spent the mornings. We never wanted to leave the sea, and getting the children into the boiling hot car for the ride home seemed such an effort. The writing was not going particularly well either, though we both tried to put in a couple of hours a day. It was easy to blame the house, but a cheat. Anyone who really wants to write can write anywhere, but it was convenient to make excuses about the house being too hot, the house being too uncomfortable, and so on. We even went so far as to tell ourselves that if we'd been in the house next door, also recently converted but lived in by the owner before being rented, then we would have been more productive. In essence, this other house was the same as ours but the difference was in how it had been furnished and decorated – a matter of taste, in short. Our owner had treated this Moorish shell as though it were a bungalow in a British suburb, whereas the owner of the next door one had chosen things that complemented the Moorish design. There were lovely textiles everywhere, and instead of sofas and chairs in the living room there was a low wooden shelf running round the room with cushions upon it as well as along the wall. The tiles on the floor were like a mosaic, and there were wall hangings embroidered with pictures of the island.

There were quite a lot of British expats living on Gozo, and it was through one of them that we heard about a house to rent in the Algarve, Portugal. This person had been there, and raved about this tiny fishing village, Praia da Luz, where this house was situated, right on the beach itself. We'd never thought of going to Portugal – didn't speak the language, for a start – and we knew very little about the Algarve, but as the heat increased during July, and being so far from the sea grew more and more irritating, we began to think about moving. We had eight months still remaining of the fourteen we had planned to be abroad and it seemed stupid to go on staying in a house we were not happy in.

So we went to Portugal, which proved as big a success as Gozo had been a mistake. Even the drive from

Faro airport along the coast road showed a more appealing landscape. Here, the countryside we passed through seemed almost empty of buildings, whereas in Gozo the land was crowded, and huge churches dominated the views. The Algarve was green, with mountains in the distance, and all the settlements along the way were of small, low stone houses with red-tiled roofs. There were few cars on the winding road but lots of horse-drawn carts, the occasional donkey being ridden by boys who waved at us. It took ages to reach Lagos, the town nearest to Praia da Luz, but long before we got there we were already sure we'd made the right decision. By the time we arrived at the village, and turned down the rough cobbled little road to the Quinta das Redes we were thinking that whatever this house turned out to be like at least its position was perfect.

We stopped outside a high wall with a green wooden door in the middle. Stepping through it was such a surprise – we had never expected the enormous garden, half of it given over to what looked like a market garden, rows and rows of cultivated vegetables, and then round the perimeter small trees that turned out to be almond and lemon. There were stone paths dividing the garden up, and a long veranda running down one side of the house which was covered in bougainvillea and vines. The house had once been a sardine factory so was in itself no architectural gem, just a one-storey stone building covering a large square area. Inside, there was one huge sitting room, a small kitchen, a bathroom and four bedrooms. It was cool and quite dark inside, though there were windows in each room, but unlike the Gozo house this was a house which had been furnished in the local style, which is to say full of Portuguese rustic pieces and fabrics. Nothing looked new. Everything was ever so slightly shabby but in an appealing way, colourful and relaxed. There were paintings on the walls, mainly of fishing boats, and a bookcase with a hundred or so books in it, all well thumbed, and a lot of them guidebooks to Portugal. On the old, scarred, wooden table there were brown glazed Portuguese plates and bowls, and the bathroom was tiled in the blue-and-white Alentejo tiles. Straw mats were laid out on the floor in the bedrooms and on the beds were the cream-coloured linen counterpanes produced locally. We could hardly believe our luck.

Settling in was easy and the writing, for both of us, picked up fast. The garden, enclosed as it was by the high wall, was perfect for four-year-old Caitlin and two-year-old Jake to be let loose in without any worries. There was actually a gardener, employed all the year round by the owners of the house, and he and the boy who worked with him didn't seem to mind the children (or if they did, they never complained). There was also a housekeeper, Fernanda. We had no choice about having her, but unlike Josephine and Lily, she was a huge asset: she cooked sometimes and she babysat occasionally in the evening when we went to see the friends we soon made. It turned out that she had been taught to cook by a man who'd rented the house for a long time, and so her repertoire was not just Portuguese dishes, none of them particularly thrilling, but French Provençale.

We had a room each to write in, another luxury. We took it in turn to have two hours with the children on the beach and two hours writing, and then in the afternoons we'd go exploring further afield. Later on, when it was not so hot, we went on expeditions up to Monchique, in the mountains, and along the coast to Sagres, the most westerly point of the Algarve. Always it was a pleasure to come home to a house which truly felt a home in spite of it being regularly rented. It was the house as much as the Algarve which we loved. We fitted in, effortlessly. There was nothing beautiful about the old building but it was solid and spacious – though, in fact, its solidity was severely tested one November night. We woke up in the early hours to hear what we thought was a lorry thundering down the track. It's going to crash, I thought, and waited for the bang as it hit the beach, but no, the thundering grew louder and nearer, and then the walls of the bedroom began to shake. We had no idea this was an earthquake until we staggered up and saw cracks appearing in the ceiling and heard glass shattering somewhere in the garden. We had no idea, either, what to do: was it better to stay inside, or rush outside? Where was most safe in an earthquake? No sooner had we realised what was happening than it was over, the only evidence that it *had* happened were the bits of plaster that had come down from the ceiling and the broken glass covering some plants in the garden. We were told later that the thing to do was to stand under an arch, and if the earthquake was a big one (how would we know?) then get away from the sea as quickly as possible. The Quinta was a pretty safe house to be in, though, unlike some of the newer houses going up in Praia da Luz which didn't have the right kind of foundations and collapsed.

There was no such risk of collapse about some houses being built, at Porto de Mos, a few miles further down the coast. These were like little Lego houses, four of them, built as a block into the hillside above the beach there, and designed by a Portuguese architect. We were taken to see them by a friend of his, who'd also become our friend, with a view to possibly buying one. If we loved the Algarve, as we'd grown to, and would definitely want to come back again and again, why not buy one of these houses instead of always renting? They were nothing like the Quinta, obviously, no rustic charm here. They were unfinished when we saw them, raw and very, very modern. But their situation was, if anything, better than the Quinta's, they had magnificent views. The Quinta had no views, enclosed as it was by the high wall. The Porto de Mos new houses were perched high on the cliff top, set slightly inland, and the view of the sea and the cliffs stretched all the way to Sagres. Then there was the beach. Whereas at Praia da Luz the beach, though pretty, was small, here the beach was enormous. It was reached from the houses by a narrow path snaking through fig trees and vines which in turn met the top of the cliff path which wound its way to the far end of the beach. There was nothing there except for a beach cafe, a wooden shack on stilts. It was all so beautiful, the wide empty beach, the lack of any buildings, the wild feeling to the whole area.

Since the houses were built into the slope of the ground, the 'front' door led into the first bedroom, which had a bathroom next to it, and then there were wooden stairs going down to the living room/kitchen, with another bedroom halfway down. This main room had sliding glass doors opening onto a broad patio with nothing in front but the path to the cliff top. Already it was easy to envisage what they would look like when completed: simple, neat – the perfect holiday house. We chose the end one in the block. Buying it was complicated (this was 1968, pre- the revolution that deposed Salazar) but it was completed two weeks before we were due to leave, though there was no time to move in. We did, though, have the chance to choose the tiles for the bathroom, and the colour of the paint, and things like that. We arranged for a bed to be made by a local carpenter, knowing how small

Portuguese beds were. Given the measurements, 6 feet by 5 feet six inches, the carpenter said what did we want, a bed or a playground? He also agreed to make wooden seating we could put cushions on, and chairs for the patio. The friend who'd taken us to see the houses agreed to supervise all this work, which, of course, we wouldn't see for many months.

On our last visit to Porto de Mos, a woman came out of the little stone house adjacent to the new houses. With her were four children, three boys and a girl, all of them staring at us eagerly. We had just enough Portuguese to understand that the woman was asking if she could be our *criada*, our maid. She was willing to do anything, to scrub – mimed vigorously – and wash clothes, anything. Her name was Emilia. She was only thirty, my age, but half her teeth were missing and she was desperately thin and worn-looking, though she smiled all the time. We said we didn't need a *criada* now, but that maybe in the future we might take her up on her offer. She smiled even more, and invited us to her house. We went over to it, and sat on a bench with the four children lined up, standing staring at us, while their mother rushed into the house to get cups of water. The cups were plastic but the water came out of a big *carafou*. We never saw the inside of the house but it was impossible not to notice the hole in the roof and the broken window and the door hanging on one hinge. Everything spoke of a hard life, but Emilia was excessively cheerful, and thrilled at the prospect of what the new houses might mean to her, and to her husband: work, money. He, she said, was useless, a drunkard, but he was strong and if we wanted a garden made he could do it. Water drunk, and our Portuguese tested to the limit, we said goodbye. Emilia and the children beamed and waved goodbye over and over. What she was really thinking, and whether the smiles vanished, the moment we were out of sight, to be replaced by an expression of resentment, we couldn't know. There was something not right about the situation, however happy Emilia had appeared to be.

But buying the Porto de Mos house made leaving to go back to London not as much of a break as it would otherwise have been. We were leaving only to come back, and we were not, in any case, as reluctant to leave as we'd thought we might be. We'd been living a false sort of existence for fourteen months, spending hours every day swimming and playing on the beach. There was no stress of the London kind, no noise or bustle, no traffic, but it was a lotus-eater kind of life. We'd got to the shocking state of thinking, as we looked at the bland blue sky, not another perfect day, half longing for the excitement of a storm and a wild wind to whip up the waves. It was humiliating to have to admit it, but this kind of life, soothing though it was, was not stimulating. For us, it lacked something. It was pleasurable, but it lacked bite – the days were simply rolling over us, hypnotic in their lack of variety. But a lesson had been learned: a way of living, many people's ideal, something to be striven for, had been proved to be not, after all, what we wanted for more than the fourteen months we'd had.

Even leaving the Quinta, a house we loved, was not too sad. It was odd that, though so content living in the Quinta, I'd regularly find myself, if I was awake in the night, imagining I was back in Boscastle Road walking up and down the stairs, counting them, and becoming puzzled when I couldn't remember if there were thirty-six or thirty-eight. And what exactly was the pattern on the hall wallpaper? Birds of some sort, but what sort, and how designed? A neighbour wrote and said how she missed our window boxes full of geraniums, which immediately made me wonder about the state of the garden. Was the grass being cut, the flowers watered? How was our house surviving?

It was time to get back to where we belonged. Living in other people's houses would not do.

Caitlin, by now five, and Jake, nearly three, had no real idea of what home was. Their memories of Boscastle Road were vague, and the house itself meant nothing to them.

But, curiously enough, once back in London, it was surprising how sharp memories of Portugal remained. In the years that followed they became devoted to the little house we'd bought, all their 'real' childhood memories seemed to be associated with it. We mostly went for a month in the summer holidays, and sometimes for a week at Easter, but once we went for Christmas too. Emilia looked after the house when we weren't there, the money she earned badly needed, and she was always eager to be helpful. That Christmas, she was adamant that she would provide a turkey. This was far too generous, but she insisted. What we hadn't realised was that the turkey would be her own, still happily running round her garden. We were invited over and she sat us in a row before emerging from her house with a cleaver. Her children chased the turkey into a corner and she butchered it there and then, the screaming awful until it was done. She then plucked it, and handed it to us, the severed neck still bloody. It was certainly organic, but it was duly eaten without enthusiasm (and there was very little meat on the bird).

HOME AGAIN

We hadn't been away from London for long enough to find it a shock landing at Heathrow Airport, with all its numbing activity, but the route to Boscastle Road was more depressing than we had remembered. No carts jogging along here, but instead a motorway clogged with heavy traffic, with drivers competing with each other as though on a race track. Row after row of tightly packed houses interspersed with factories, and enormous shopping centres, and everywhere bold and garish signs proclaiming the names of brands of goods. Hardly any greenery for the majority of the way, and the sense, all the time, of a tight compression, of there not being a single metre of spare space.

At least when we got to the top of Highgate Hill

there was some relief, with trees visible over the rooftops, and when at last we turned into our road it was as quiet as it had always been. I was nervous entering our house, prepared to find nothing looked right, and that I would feel a stranger, and maybe that I might even not like the house any more after the splendour of the Quinta, and what would I do then? And it did feel strange, nothing in its place, though everything was clean and tidy. But this strangeness was not so much to do with how the furniture was arranged as with the size of the rooms. I'd thought them spacious, but after the Quinta they seemed cramped. I moved restlessly about, literally repossessing my territory, not at all sure that I was as intimately acquainted with this house as I'd thought I was.

Then Mrs Hall appeared, newly returned from another visit to her daughter in America and so sure that it would be her last that she was just going to stay at home from now on. We took the news badly. Never mind the sudden apparent smallness of the rooms – much worse was this reminder that we were back to sharing our house. The time had surely come: either Mrs Hall had to go, or we did. Maybe now we could persuade her to move out.

The plan was to buy a flat for her to rent from us at the same rate as she was already paying, and which would be hers to rent for the rest of her life. Rather nervously, not at all sure what her response would be, we put this to her. Her first reaction was that we might be cheating her. How could she be sure she would be as protected in another flat as she was in our house, because of being a sitting tenant, and having the law on her side? She said she'd have to go down to the Citizens Advice Bureau and have any agreement checked legally. Fine by us. Then came the conditions: this flat must be within certain boundaries strictly drawn up by her. Kentish Town as far as the polytechnic would be acceptable, but not Tufnell Park. The boundary there was Dartmouth Park Hill, and on the other side, Highgate Road. She would also have to consult her daughters and she warned us that one of them had 'worked for Churchill' and knew 'what was what'.

But we could tell that she was keen on the idea, realising perfectly well that the thirty-eight stairs up to her flat in our house were soon going to be too much for her and she'd have to move anyway. So the hunt was on. It was by then 1969 and our area, in a mere six years, had become more desirable. There were fewer flats available as houses were being bought and converted by families, and those that still existed were often at the top of the house, just like Mrs Hall's existing flat, and therefore had to be ruled out because of the stairs. But we saw that a new block was being built in Swains Lane, the northern boundary of Mrs Hall's permitted streets. This block of eight flats was near a bus terminus, opposite shops, and across the road from the Heath. She was not as enthusiastic as we'd thought she would be, but said she'd look at a flat there when it was finished and consider it. But she didn't want a ground floor flat, in spite of the condition of her legs. It must be on the first floor, so that nosy parkers couldn't look in or burglars gain easy entry. Negotiations began, of various sorts, and eventually the deal was done. The flat cost more than our house had done but turned out to be a good investment.

It was an attractive flat, everything in it new and sparkling. Mrs Hall had the grace to be delighted with it, especially since she now had her own ultra-modern bathroom (alas, the blue rubber bath stickers never got transferred) and a proper kitchen. She had a bedroom and a sitting room, with a little balcony where she could have plant pots, and it was all on one floor. The stairs up to it were few in number and shallow, so she would be able to manage them for a long time (as she did, for twelve years). Best of all was an intercom system, so she could check who was ringing her bell without having actually to go to the door. The daughter who lived in England came to help her move and was fulsome with her praise, telling her mother how lucky she'd been. Mrs Hall was not prepared to go quite that far. 'Boscastle Road was my home,' she said, piously, 'this will never be home in the same way.' Considering she'd only lived in it for thirteen of her seventy-two years, this sentiment seemed not a little extravagant. She left our house in dramatic fashion, wiping the tears away and waving her hand, as though to a person.

The deed done, we were free to do what we'd been longing to do for years: make the ground floor into one big through room. J.P. Brown was not available to do this job (the wind had got him by then) so we hired a new builder, who worked only with his two sons. It was quite challenging work, involving a RSJ, a giant concrete girder, being put across the centre of the new space, so there was a lot of dirt and dust again while the dividing wall came down and the RSJ went up. The marble fireplace was taken out, and the bookshelves we had built into the two alcoves now joined into one. Light came flooding in from both ends and all feeling of being cramped had gone. Meanwhile, on the top floor we had Mrs Hall's kitchen converted into a bedroom, and a bathroom put in on the landing. The children, now almost seven and five, moved upstairs and had a bedroom each, with a spare room ready for all our many visiting Carlisle relations.

We hadn't yet had either my parents, or my widowed mother-in-law to stay, though our brothers and sisters had all visited while the house was still in a poor state. Our parents, we knew, found our house a disappointment. A Victorian house was not their idea of what a house should be: too many stairs, rooms that were too big, ceilings that were too high, etc. My brother's smart semi-detached house in Stanwix, Carlisle, was their ideal house. At least the garden met with approval, though my father was scandalised that so much ground was given to grass when it could've been used to grow potatoes. My mother-in-law's only comment was that there was plenty of room for lodgers.

So there we were, the house transformed and now truly ours. The sense of freedom, with Mrs Hall gone, was terrific. We were settled.

There I was, in the early seventies, serene in my house, serene enough to want another baby. Flora was born in

October 1972, soon after I'd finished my first attempt at a biography (of Bonnie Prince Charlie). Our house was full, and busy.

Once Flora was born there was little time for writing. I still managed an hour in the mornings, my preferred time, while she slept, but after that, I was walking on the Heath with her then collecting Caitlin and Jake from school, often bringing their friends home too. From then on it was all hectic activity, and then time to feed everyone. Write later on, after Hunter was home? Impossible. I was too tired to even think of lifting a pen. Sometimes I read of other women writers, in my situation, who had gone to hotels, or rented rooms, to write in, and I couldn't believe it – without being in my own house I knew I wouldn't be able to write at all. The surroundings were everything. I managed, though, with scraps of time. I was happy doing it.

But the house, in three years' time, was about to change its meaning for me, to become a refuge in a manner I'd never imagined.

It is too dreary to catalogue all the details of the cancer (I refuse to personalise the disease, though it is a very personal one, by calling it 'my' cancer) which began, or showed itself, in 1975. I remember them all, of course, all too clearly, but everyone by now is surely familiar with the breast cancer scenario: the finding of a lump, the diagnosis, the biopsy, the operation, etc. The cancer I was discovered to have resulted in a mastectomy in April 1975, at the Royal Free Hospital in Hampstead. It was a very small lump, of low grade, and no radiotherapy was thought necessary. The consultant I was treated by, a Miss George, was abrupt and impatient in manner. She wheeled in her team in a military manner, and gave them an on-the-spot lecture, going through all the reasons why I was an unlikely candidate for breast cancer – age (thirty-six), breast-fed three children for nine months each, fit, non-smoker – saying that this was probably a 'one off', just 'bad luck'.

Probably. What a sinister word. I analysed its meaning over and over again, coming up with a new inter-pretation each time. I was still thinking about my own invented law of probability when the surgical appliance woman came to talk about a prosthesis to replace the missing breast, assuring me that once I had it I would be 'as good as new' and in no time at all I'd probably get so used to it I'd hardly notice the difference. Laughing hurt, what with the drains still in and the dressing still on the wound, so I had to restrain myself. Then I lay there thinking about how curious it was that the whole emphasis was on how I would *look*, not how I would feel or how I would cope with knowing I had the disease. I was lucky to be able to ruminate in peace, because through a fluke I had a room of my own (it wasn't needed at the time and nobody else wanted it). I tried to treat this room as a room in my house. I was allowed to tape the children's drawings to the walls, and on the shelf running under the window I had some of my books, and small items brought in from home. The nurses weren't too keen on my beloved fountain pen in case it leaked ink, so I switched to biro, and tried to make my bed like my desk.

All these attempts failed to create the atmosphere of my house. I tried to tell myself that a hospital is just a house, if a big one, a house with many rooms and corridors. It has a roof over it, and walls, lots of walls, protecting the inmates from rain and cold, a good place to be in. But for me, it wasn't. I wanted to be in my own house, where I knew I would heal quicker. Arriving home was in itself a healing process. Once I was inside my house the relief washed over me like a tide going out – I was on dry land again, secure within its familiar walls. And that's how the house changed its significance for me. It took on a magical quality: if I stayed in my house, I'd be safe. I knew perfectly well that this was fanciful nonsense, but it was how I felt. Sometimes, in the weeks that followed, I'd be out on the Heath enjoying a walk when I'd be overwhelmed with an urgent need to be inside my house. I'd start walking more quickly, then almost run, and when I reached our front door my hand would fumble with the key in my haste to get into the house. Once inside, I'd stand for a moment with my back against the door, and the ordinary sight of the staircase ahead of me, a toy dropped halfway up, a basket of clean clothes lying on the bottom stair waiting to be taken up – all this would calm me. I was fine again, cocooned by the familiarity of the house.

I'd been told to 'forget' about the cancer and 'get on with your life'. I didn't forget, ever, but I certainly got on with my life. Part of this getting on was embarking on a biography of W.M. Thackeray (which later turned into a pretend autobiography). I was well, had readjusted to life with one breast. The only exception was when I had to leave the house for check-ups. The clinic was always crowded, the wait long, some of those waiting clearly in pain. It was impossible not to hear what people were saying to their companions (nearly everyone took someone with them for support, though I never did) and much of this overheard conversation was frightening. Women would reminisce about what they'd been told – 'the doctor told me it was only a Grade 1, you don't need radiotherapy' – and then launch into 'and now it's in my bones, and that Miss George, she says to the other doctor, it's an adverse prognosis, she thinks I'm thick and don't know what it means.' Mostly, the women attending these clinics were patient and resigned, but others were loudly bitter and resentful, claiming none of the questions they had were ever answered, that is if they were even given an opportunity to ask them. They'd mention, too, articles they'd read in newspapers or magazines, some of which maintained that nobody knew what they were doing in the breast cancer field and then would follow lots of depressing statistics. Clinic days in the seventies were bad days, even when I emerged unscathed.

It struck me that if, as many claim, the body is merely a house for the spirit and the mind, then its owner has to keep up constant surveillance. Before I found that minuscule lump, and I only found it because I was following widely publicised instructions for women to do a regular checking of their breasts, I had had no symptoms of cancer, therefore why believe that feeling fine meant there was no need to worry? Of course there was. My own vigilance had found that lump so it was up to me to be vigilant all the time. This proved exhausting, enough to turn anyone into a nervous wreck. 'Forgetting' was ridiculous, especially with the visible reminder of what had happened. Nor was it helpful for people to talk about 'fighting' cancer, and being 'positive' in attitude. There is no fighting that can be done, and being positive not only has no proven effect but it creates another psychological burden for the patient. Better to accept that, if indeed the body is a kind of house, then this house has a touch of woodworm, or dry rot, or similar, which may be treated to a certain degree but it won't ever be certain that it has all been eradicated. Maybe, in those rafters at the top of this house, or in one of those floorboards at the bottom, there is just a tiny, tiny bit left which, given the encouragement of the right conditions, will start travelling again through the rest of the house which had seemed up to that point perfectly clear of damage. So, that was my reading of the situation I was in.

We had at the time, while all this was happening, a weekend cottage in Upper Wardington, Northamptonshire. The

Heath was lovely, but it was no substitute for the real countryside, and at weekends it gets busy, so we thought we'd escape London every Friday–Monday and enjoy the delights of living among fields and having long walks. It wasn't what could be termed a yummy Cotswolds-type cottage, but it was situated at the end of a lane, on the fringe of the village, and it had a large garden with nothing overlooking it.

We had it four years, long enough to find out that weekending was not for us, and especially not for me. I loved being there, but I didn't love the coming and going, and once cancer entered the equation this became too much. Every Friday, picking Caitlin and Jake, aged eight and six, up from school and zooming off up the M1, to beat the rush, I'd be thinking how tiring all this was, all the preparation that went into it, and then every Sunday evening, or very early Monday morning, I'd be thinking why on earth are we leaving just as we've got settled and it's so quiet and lovely here. I felt, too, faithless to both houses. Which did I prefer? Or which situation did I prefer? And if the answer to that one was 'the country' why didn't we move there and find a house as roomy as Boscastle Road? Such a luxury, having that option. But one of them, one of these houses, had to go.

My state of health hastened the decision to give the cottage up, but a burglary at Boscastle Road helped too. This wasn't like the burglary while I was living in Richardson Street, but a much more thorough job. We'd made it very easy for the burglars. All they'd had to do was break down a thin temporary plywood door at the back of the house, where yet more alterations were being made to extend the kitchen during the Easter holidays. Once inside, the burglars stayed there cosily for (it was reckoned by the police) two days, sleeping and eating there while they did their work in a leisurely fashion. At one point, the au pair girl across the road had seen someone drawing the curtains. Thinking it was a friend of ours, she gave a cheerful wave, and this person waved happily back.

It was the sight of the mess, of course, which was shocking, rather than what turned out to be missing. The burglars' method of searching had been to turn out every drawer and cupboard and then kick their way through the resulting heaps of stuff to see if anything of value turned up. There was no cash in the house, which probably didn't improve their temper, and though we by then had a television it was only a small black and white one. Once we'd sorted through the chaos, it emerged very little had been taken – a carriage clock, a radio, a silver box. I had no jewellery of value, other than a coral necklace, which had been tipped out of its box and left. But it was strange that two vividly coloured crocheted blankets, made by my mother-in-law for the children's beds, had also gone. They'd been used, the police reckoned, to wrap something in. That 'something' turned out to be every one of Hunter's Beatles LPs, including *Sergeant Pepper*, the sleeve signed by all four Beatles. (I do hope the burglars hung on to them. That *Sergeant Pepper* one would today be worth £57,000.)

No house in our street had, at that time (1976) a burglar alarm, though quite soon afterwards they started appearing. Ours was a nuisance, endlessly going off for no reason, making us unpopular with neighbours. But though we no longer went away every weekend, once the cottage was sold, we were out of London all the school holidays. Most of these, apart from a month in the Algarve, were spent in Carlisle, visiting our parents. Neither my parents, nor my mother-in-law, could put all five of us up, so we had to split ourselves between their two bungalows. We thought that if we had a small cottage somewhere on the fells, near enough to go backwards and forwards to Carlisle in half an hour or so, then it would make spending the holidays up there a lot easier. It wouldn't be like week-ending, because we'd be there for mostly two-week periods.

We bought a tiny, one-up, one-down cottage outside Caldbeck, twelve miles from Carlisle. It was a wreck, far more of a wreck than Boscastle Road had been. Built in the eighteenth century, it was said to have been lived in by the famous huntsman, John Peel. It was out on the fells, in wild countryside, off an unfenced road and up a track which, in rain, turned into a bog. The term 'in need of modernisation' was this time literally true, with no kitchen, no bathroom, a dirt floor, and a hole in the roof. Beside this cottage was a broken down barn, one half of a wall missing. Thirteen acres of land went with it, and a stream ran through the edge of this area.

It was exactly what we wanted.

But the timing was wrong. We bought the cottage in 1977. The renovations were going to take six months, but before they were completed, and the cottage was ready to inhabit, I was once more in hospital. This time, the cancer was more serious, and I was in the Royal Marsden, not the Royal Free (my GP, who had been on holiday the first time, was adamant: at that time, the Marsden was the best). Nobody, after this second mastectomy, in January 1978, was any longer talking about this being a 'one-off' thing. The tumour was small, but the cancer had spread to two of the twenty lymph nodes, and after a second mastectomy I was to be given chemotherapy for six months. I would be part of a random trial, in which a computer would decide whether the drug would be delivered intravenously, in which case my hair would fall out, or by tablets, in which case I'd be sick. The computer drew the tablet-form for me, which was a relief, though not because of anything to do with losing my hair but because it meant I could be in my own house.

The Marsden experience was grim. It was under-going refurbishment at the time, so some wards were closed, meaning that others, including the one I was in, were overcrowded. Patients who were dying were mixed in with the rest of us who were not in such a dire state. There was no question of having a room on my own – I was lucky to have a bed to myself – and it was ludicrous to try to pretend that the hospital was a house I could adapt to my needs. It was an institution, struggling magnificently to do the best it could, and it felt like one. But on the plus side, I had a friendly, sympathetic and humane surgeon, Mr

McKinna, who seemed to work twenty-four hours a day, every day, but always had time to chat. He had a lively registrar, too, an American on a six-month placement from a New York hospital, who appeared shocked by the aftercare for breast cancer patients, though he could see no difference between the two countries in the surgical treatment.

It was harder, much harder, to adjust this time, and not only because of the implications of the looming chemotherapy. There was a patient in our ward dying of brain cancer. She was in a screened-off part of the ward but, of course, it wasn't soundproof, and so all night long we heard the poor woman calling out 'the pain, the pain, the pain', and then 'move me, turn me, turn me, help me, help me', and then the screaming began. There was nothing any of us could do, but one night we were all appalled to hear a nurse shout, 'Shut up! Turn yourself, if you want.' This same nurse then came round the ward, telling each of us not to upset ourselves, and that this woman needed 'disciplining'. When she'd finished her round, she went back to the moaning patient and said, 'Now be quiet, you're upsetting the other patients and behaving like a spoiled baby.' No one slept after that. I struggled to calm myself, knowing it would be a mistake to appear 'overwrought', and so not trustworthy, and asked to see the Sister, to report what we'd all heard. She listened carefully and said she would deal with it. We never saw the nurse in question again, so presumably it was an agency nurse.

The day I started the chemotherapy, I was still in the Marsden. In the next cubicle, the green and blue curtains drawn, a priest was reciting the last rites over one patient; further down the ward, another priest was reciting them over the brain tumour patient, now quiet; across the ward, a much younger priest was talking to an Irish girl as six of her relatives listened with her, all in tears. None of the priests acknowledged each other. It was a suitably solemn atmosphere in which to pop the little white pill in my mouth, wondering whether in a hundred years' time this drug would be looked back on as poison, or useless, or as a great life saver. My ignorance was total. I couldn't have any part in the decision to have chemotherapy, because I had no medical knowledge at all. I couldn't have weighed the pros and cons. There had to be trust in the doctor with no chance of being in any kind of control. Fortunately, Mr McKinna inspired trust. He explained that he simply had no way of knowing, not just if the chemo would work, but whether it was actually necessary, though he thought it was.

'Two tumours in three years and other areas found to be active plus a spread, if a small one, to the lymph glands, means I can't take the chance. If I'm wrong, I'll have put you through an unpleasant experience for nothing, but I don't think I am wrong.'

I went home the next day, but not straight home. Out of bravado, and because it was a glorious winter's day, Hunter drove me from the Marsden to Kenwood, on the Heath, and we walked round the west meadow. It was bitterly cold, but the sky was bright, blue and cloudless, and over the grass was a slight mist hovering, about to lift. I felt like an escaped convict, OUT at last, free. Then we went home, and going home felt even better than being out. It was extraordinary that an ordinary Victorian house should have the power to make me feel so relieved and happy, but it did. I loved everything about it from the moment I went back through the front door, saw the pattern of the wallpaper, and the pictures on the walls and the big glass mirror with its gilt frame and the long pine shelf underneath it and then into the living room with its orange-covered sofas and the big pine table and all the jumble of books and belongings, all of it so familiar and yet a shock, the shock of identifying with it all, knowing it all had *meaning*. In our bedroom, the pleasure of being in my own bed was intense, lying there, looking at the pale yellow-and-white William Morris wallpaper and the Sheila Fell painting of a field at harvest time and the Clarice Cliff bowl on the shelf below it and the framed family photographs on the other wall, and out of the window the bare black branches of the giant plane tree in a nearby garden stretching into the sky. I kept falling asleep then waking again, checking it was all true, that I was home, *in my house*, thrilled to be there, knowing that now I could begin to recover and heal.

There was a lot to heal, and the house couldn't do all of it. The psychological battle to be 'normal' exhausted me. I felt physically out of proportion now that I'd had another mastectomy, as though my body was concave, one strange sweep inwards from chin to waist, and only then resuming its usual dimensions. I walked differently, seeming to lean slightly backwards, as though to balance better, which was ridiculous. And I took to shrouding myself in smock-like shirts, still battling with the decision of whether to be fitted with prosthesis. A double mastectomy changed everything, making it no longer possible to convince myself that in order not to look lopsided, and draw attention to myself, I had no choice about wearing a prosthesis. I had a choice now. I wouldn't be lopsided, just completely flat-chested, no need to wear those stupid things as if I were some kind of drag artist. But vanity – or was it vanity? – pulled me the other way. If I submitted to these substitute breasts (which had begun to improve in shape and texture by then) might it not make me feel as well as look 'normal'? I wished it was the 1920s, the era when the look was flat-chested for every woman.

I paid a macabre visit to a little room in Clifford Street, off Bond Street, where two smiling, white-coated, highly made-up women ran a patient care service, funded by God knows who. They were surrounded by boxes of false breasts, piled up beneath certificates on the walls for every variety of surgical appliances, with barely room to move, what with their desk and a trolley and an electric kettle in front of which sat three jars of instant coffee and a box of tea bags. They were so proud of their wares, pulling out breast after breast, demonstrating the different shapes, and then politely asking if I could 'see' myself in any of them. Once it stopped being revolting it became, or I became, hysterical. It was like pretending we were having a cosy conversation about woolly gloves, discussing the size, the weight, the fabric. I decided to try the 'very latest model', which looked quite alarmingly nasty, but these women waxed lyrical about it, vowing I'd hardly know the difference from real skin. This type, they pointed out, was hollow, therefore virtually weightless, and it stuck to the chest. They couldn't wait to fit two onto me, and they managed to do this with ease and affection, though I cringed, only managing not to run screaming from the room by repeating to myself my mantra of 'better than a false leg, better than a false leg'. Straight afterwards, I went to Russell & Bromley's and bought a pair of beautifully shiny, bright-red Wellingtons. Better than a false leg, better than a false leg . . .

I still felt, though, that I was wrong, stupid, to have, as it were, given in. Why pretend to have breasts when I no longer had them? Did it make me less of a woman? Does being a woman mean you have to have breasts? I spent idle hours imagining all the women I admired suddenly having no breasts, and then even more bizarrely imagining famous beauties with no breasts – ah, but there a difference had to be admitted. Marilyn Monroe was not Marilyn Monroe without these pieces of flesh, a cleavage was essential. I became temporarily obsessed with looking at every woman I met and removing her breasts, just to see how this changed her. It was fascinating to discover women who could take this removal easily and hardly suffer from it, and those who were diminished, and whose breasts I had quickly to restore. It was a game I played to extinction in those first few weeks, but it was harmless because nobody knew what I was doing.

Meanwhile, the physical recovery went on, and so did the chemotherapy. I wasn't sick. The experience wasn't unpleasant, except for the extreme tiredness, but then most women with three young children are tired anyway. I had regular blood tests, to check that the white blood cell count hadn't fallen too low because of the chemo. In mid-February, when these tests were satisfactory and I was feeling strong enough, we decided, at long last, to go and inspect the Caldbeck cottage where almost all the renovations had been completed. Hunter was doing a book about the Lake District at the time so he was combining work with this visit, and set off first by car. I followed by train three days later, with my sister-in-law looking after the children. We'd had arguments before he left, about the contents of the car. He'd promised me that this Caldbeck cottage really would be a butt and ben, not in any way a proper home, and would be kept spare and minimal, which it needed to be anyway because it was so tiny. But he'd packed the car with things

he thought might 'come in useful', as well as things I'd
bought for the cottage. These included an old cane bed
head, a worn-out looking hosepipe, two stone jars that
'might' be made into lamps, six empty coffee jars, a rug his
mother had given us which I'd always hated, and a stool
which had the strands of its wickerwork top frayed.

The train journey to Windermere seemed the height
of excitement to me – that feeling again of being out,
released, escaped. Only six weeks since I'd left the Marsden
and here I was, able to board a train and go off for the
weekend. We stayed in a hotel that night and then the next
morning drove to the cottage. It was like going into a fairy
tale. Lifting the latch on the wooden door and walking in
I wasn't sure if I was little Red Riding Hood, expecting to
see the wolf posing as her granny, or one of the Three Bears
returning home, shocked to see their bowls empty. The
minute room was full of little compositions, all asking to
be painted, from the one small window, the red curtains
I'd made framing it, to the old original fireplace taking up
all of one wall and laden with logs. The floor now had
stone flags, and the thick walls were plastered and painted
white. A table covered in red-and-white gingham stood
under the window and a two-seater, narrow sofa was

squeezed into the remaining space. There was no real kitchen, just an alcove off this main room, with a stone sink and next to it a cooker. Stone stairs, uncovered and steep, led to a bedroom on one side and a narrow box room on the other. The bathroom was a marvel, somehow fitted under these stairs. There was nothing to do but admire.

This cottage had been built to withstand the full force of the wild winds coming from the west and so it was dug low into the ground. There were only two small windows – one in the living room one in the bedroom. Not much could be seen from them but views were not the point: keeping the wind and cold out was more important. That first night, there was a tremendous wind, howling and roaring all around, but the cottage stood firm, not a rattle to be heard. It hunkered down, just as it had done for two hundred years, and being inside it felt secure and safe. Not so outside. It was a shock, next morning, to step outside and feel the wind, though by then it had quietened down a good deal. We set off to walk on the top fell road above Caldbeck, where the rough land sweeps down to the fells beyond, and some of the trees are so pushed by the wind that they appear almost horizontal, level with the ground. There was a rainbow above us, held up, it seemed, by thick buffeting clouds on either side, acting as buttresses. The sense of space was vast, miles and miles of green, with sheep everywhere and in the distance a group of fell ponies wandered backwards and forwards across the unfenced road.

It wasn't difficult, once back in the cottage, to imagine what life had been like for those living there before us. Everything about living there had been hard, involving exhausting physical labour of one sort or another. Simply keeping the fire going – for warmth, for cooking – meant an endless gathering of wood. It ate wood. All the logs we'd had delivered seemed to be burned in no time. The fireplace itself was so huge it needed half a forest to keep it going, and if the fire in it went out the cold was intense. Getting up in the morning, starting the fire was a priority, but it was unlikely those living here, who worked as farmers, would have bothered. It would be straight out in the morning, with no hot drink or food, unless the fire still had an ember or two which could be quickly coaxed into burning. The privy was round the back, and any washing would have to be done with a bucket of water taken from the rain barrel. By comparison, we were living here in the height of luxury and comfort, and we were well aware of it.

Leaving the cottage, which was so snug and enclosed, it was always surprising to be reminded that there was an outside world in which we were a mere blip. The few farm buildings we could see looked insignificant against the landscape. What dominated were the fells, with High Pike the highest. I wanted to climb it, in spite of the wind. Climbing High Pike is not like climbing mountains such as Skiddaw, where there are well-marked paths. The ground here is rough and full of peat hags, and there are no paths. The climber makes her own way, the best way she can. It was gruelling that day, with my energy low and the weather against me, but I was determined to do it to show myself I could. Reaching the top of High Pike isn't particularly rewarding either, there isn't the thrill of standing on the summit of Helvellyn or Scafell, though the view across the Eden Valley to the Pennines can be exhilarating. Not that day, though. Cloud came down, the rain began, and we could see very little. When we got back to the haven that was the cottage, I was shattered. I'd hated the climb, hated the slogging on, the struggle not to be blown sideways by the vicious wind, hated having fallen into the must-get-to-the-top trap when it wasn't in the least important to do so.

That night, there was a violent storm, making the

wind of the day before seem nothing. The rain was not like normal rain, like city rain, but more like an avalanche of water, thundering against the windows, making a noise as though rocks were being hurled against them. This was another version of a house as a place of refuge, this time from the elements – its original purpose. Surely the glass in the windows would crack, surely the tiles on the roof would blow off. Yet in the morning, when we nervously went to inspect the damage outside, there was no evidence of a terrible revenge wreaked by the storm. Some branches of trees were broken off, and the potholes in the track leading to the road were full of water, but otherwise there was no sign that there'd been a storm at all. The cottage sat smugly, knowing it had survived worse many times.

Our last night there, all was quiet, intensely quiet, after the storm. The black all round the cottage was dense, unrelieved by any light from a moon or stars. When we put the lamp off inside, just to experiment, to see how dark it really was, and slowly walked a few yards away from the door, it felt perilous. There was nothing for us to bump into, so we counted twenty paces, without being able to see where we were going, and then turned round to count those twenty steps back to the door. We got nowhere near it. Putting our hands out to feel the door, or the wall, there was nothing there. Opening and shutting our eyes made no difference. The black was the same. We shuffled around cautiously till we found we had reached the gate, which meant we'd gone in entirely the wrong direction and were about ten yards from the cottage. Getting back to it was a matter of blindly inching slowly forwards.

Before we left the next day, we made lists of what we needed to bring when we came for the Easter holidays with the children. A torch was number one.

CHANGING TIMES

The 1980s

It took nine months, not the planned six, for me to be finished with the chemotherapy, because of my white blood cell count once falling low enough to mean there had to be a halt till it climbed back up again. Once this treatment was over, and I'd been checked out at the Marsden, we began thinking of one final alteration to our house.

At this point we could have moved back to Hampstead, with the value of our Boscastle Road house now sufficient to finance it. Hunter was keen, though partly his enthusiasm was to do with his love not just of looking at houses but bidding for them. He had his eye on Downshire Hill and dragged me off to inspect houses there on four different occasions – dragged, because I didn't want to move. I loved my existing house more and more, and I valued the neighbourhood, where we were deeply embedded. My ordinary house in an ordinary road on the wrong side of the Heath had become special to me. So, as an alternative to the excitement of moving, we decided to incorporate the yard, between the little room that had been the coalhouse and the kitchen, into the fabric of the house, making a new room out of this space which would have glass doors opening onto the garden. At the same time, another room would be added on top of the bathroom, which would be Hunter's office now that he worked mainly at home.

All around us during this period, people were moving into the area and doing the same kind of thing. Every road seemed to have at least two skips in it as the houses were disembowelled, and bricks and plaster and bits of wood and old pipes were heaped into them. Walls were knocked down, back additions rebuilt, lofts made into rooms. Half the houses in our road had had bed-sitting rooms in them when we arrived in 1963, but by now – in 1980 – they had almost entirely disappeared. The demolition of the interiors was followed by an army of decorators, set to make the houses modern and attractive. The road became crowded with vans, painters, plumbers and electricians, vying for space. Every day except Sunday (and sometimes on Sunday too) the noise of hammering and drilling and sawing could be heard, one strong hum of energy vibrating along the road. NW5 was clearly no longer on the wrong side of Hampstead Heath, no longer Hampstead's poor relation.

Then one day, the house next door to us, our semi-detached neighbour, was sold. Previously, an elderly couple had lived there, a quiet self-contained pair who, though they kept their garden immaculate, had done nothing to their house in all the many years they'd lived there. They went off to a bungalow in Bournemouth and their house was sold immediately to a man who was rumoured to own several other houses. He apparently bought in order to modernise, and then sell at a huge profit. It didn't sound like good news for us. We'd grown used to our pleasant neighbours and would've liked them to stay. But we'd altered our own house so we could hardly complain about the noise that now went on as the next door house was ripped apart and put together differently.

The owner who eventually moved in next door seemed to live there with a constantly changing group of other people. He wasn't interested in any kind of neigh-bourliness and could barely bring himself to say hello as he came and went. Fine, that was the way he wanted it. But this lack of any recognition made it hard to deal with what began to happen in this house, often when he himself was not there. His friends, if 'friends' was an apt descrip-tion, were fond of flinging open the windows so that the excruciating loud beat of their music could blast over the garden in the early hours of the morning. More alarming, sometimes one of them would crouch smoking on the windowsill, above the glass roof of the new exten-sion, and once we were horrified to see a man hanging by his fingertips from this windowsill, dangling over the glass before hands appeared to grab his arms and haul him back in. To add to the fun, there was an Alsatian dog that raced up and down the garden barking furiously, and once a woman in a white dress ran screaming from the house, throwing her arms up in what looked like appeal. Just as we grabbed the phone to call the police, she stopped screaming and began laughing hysterically, and when a man came out she flung herself at him and he wrapped her in an embrace and she kissed him and then they went back inside, apparently devoted to each other.

There were several years of this kind of thing, with the loud music played all night being the hardest to endure. We tried making polite objections, saying we didn't want to be unreasonable but could the music be lowered after midnight, especially in the room next to our bedroom? This was always agreed to, with a 'yeah, sure', but the tremendous noise went on. Just as we reached the point of thinking we'd have to see if there was any law against this kind of torment, there would be a sudden cessation of all sound. We'd see an exodus from the house, of about a dozen people, all carrying bags and piles of belongings, and getting into battered vans. For as long as a whole month there would be blessed silence, and then a new lot would arrive, in twos and threes, until the house was once more full again and the same sort of noise would begin.

All those years of living next to a quiet, considerate elderly couple we had smugly imagined that our Victorian house, unlike modern houses, had thick walls, which insulated it from noise. Wrong. Well built or not, the dividing walls between our house and next door hardly dulled the music. The walls in certain rooms seemed to vibrate, or so we imagined, and we'd stare at paintings hanging on these walls, expecting them to crash to the floor at any moment. Sometimes, in desperation, we'd thump on the walls to register our objection. This proved ridiculous. If our thumps were heard at all, they were ignored, or more likely treated as a joke. Once at two in the morning, when the whole of our house seemed invaded by the relentless beat coming from next door, Hunter went and hammered on the front door, determined to at least try a face-to-face appeal. It was eventually opened by a young man he'd never seen before who beamed and stood aside to let him in, welcome to the party, make yourself at home. He found the ground floor room full of people lying there stoned, completely immobile, raising only a hand in greeting but making no objection when, locating the stereo, he turned the volume right down. No one was aggressive, no one asked what the hell he thought he was doing. Pleased with his apparently easy victory, he came back to bed. Five minutes later, the music was back, louder than ever.

So, our house was not invulnerable. We'd learned the obvious truth that a semi-detached house, of whatever age, and however stoutly built, is always at the mercy of those in the house attached to it. If it had not been for our regular escape during all the school holidays, to our Caldbeck bolt-hole, and our Algarve summer house, I don't know how we would have survived all this noise. It was bliss to get to Caldbeck where the only sound in the night was the sheep coughing or the wind in the trees. Our only neighbour was a woman who lived a hundred yards away in another cottage from which no sound ever came. She lived an entirely secluded life, wanting nothing to do with us, but seeming to enjoy watching our children play. She'd look out of her window and smile and wave at them: the perfect neighbour. We wished we could transport her to Boscastle Road and have her there too, living next door.

Then one day, without any estate agent's board going up, we heard a rumour that next door had been sold. The house market had taken another leap upwards and the owner had grabbed his chance. People were still coming and going, the noise was still the same, so we couldn't believe anything was going to change. But it was. A great silence descended. Silence all day silence all night, no movement anywhere. There were several weeks when nothing seemed to be happening, and we waited anxiously to find out what our fate would be. Another property speculator? More than likely. The relief when a family with three children moved in made us light-headed. All our neighbour troubles faded away. From then on, the next door house changed occupants several times, but no one ever again ruined the peace and quiet of our house.

Other things did, though. Houses, of course, deteriorate just like bodies in old age. In spite of all the maintenance work that had been done on it, ours started to show signs of collapse. Cracks began appearing in the wall between the large ground floor room and the newly extended kitchen come living room. Each month they got wider until it was possible to stick a finger into the main crack which snaked right across the wall from top to bottom. The builder was called in. We hoped he'd dismiss the cracks as just plaster settling down, but he didn't. He called in someone else, who also looked grave, and called in a third person to give their opinion. Even though the comparison was outrageously inappropriate, there were faint echoes of waiting for certain medical news . . . it would be bad. It was. The trouble, we were told, was subsidence. Subsidence? Apparently, this meant that our house was sinking at the back. If something were not done, the back wall would collapse. When? How long would it take? Hard to say, but if we were hoping that the answer might be . . . oh, maybe in another 50 years and we might outlive this event, and so need do nothing, we were mistaken. Something had to be done, something drastic, and at once.

'Something drastic' meant having a pit dug across the width of the back room and then having it filled with concrete. Nothing else would do. So the pristine new wooden floor was levered up in great chunks and the drills put to work. It was horrible to watch and the mess appalling. We had the area barricaded off, and a temporary kitchen made, but the thunderous roar of the drills could not be shut out. The whole house shuddered and tensed itself, and more and more images of it being a gravely sick body sprang to my mind. Many people move out of their houses when subsidence work is going on, but we didn't want to leave ours even though it meant enduring the noise and dirt. I thought of films I'd seen of houses in the Blitz, and told myself this was not nearly so bad, only part of the house was being damaged and soon it would be made good. Only it wasn't 'soon'. It took a long time before the required depth was reached and the builder was ready to pour in the concrete.

We couldn't resist doing the *Blue Peter* thing: burying a time capsule underneath the concrete. We got a biscuit box and filled it with information about who was living in the house, and what was going on in London and the world. Good fun. A newspaper was the obvious first thing to put in, and then photographs of us all, together with a detailed plan of the interior of the house and how each room was used. We added a tape of currently popular music and a signed photograph of the Tottenham Hotspur team together with a programme for the match played the previous Saturday. We each added one small item of significance to us but nobody else, to intrigue and puzzle rather than inform. I put in a fountain pen I'd just had to give up using after twenty years because the nib had sprung. That should baffle them – in a hundred years nobody might still be using an ink pen. We liked imagining what anyone finding this box in the distant future would think (but had a dreadful fear that the subsidence work would have failed and we'd find the box ourselves, all too soon, when the whole thing had to be done again).

Everything was eventually put back as it had been, but we were nervous for a long time. It had been a reminder that bricks and mortar are not as solid as they look. Nothing about a house remains solid. We were only just beginning to learn that maintenance work never stops, something that may be obvious but it hadn't been to us. And it needs a certain attitude of mind to cope with the loads of things to do with looking after a house which need attention, the bodily equivalent of regular haircutting, teeth-filling and so on. We didn't have the right attitude. We moaned and groaned every time there was a leaking pipe, or a faulty electrical connection or a tile came off the roof. A house, our beloved house, was then in danger of becoming a nuisance, something we were close to resenting because it took up too much time to look after. We had to remind ourselves that we were very, very grateful to have a house at all.

There are, of course, and always have been, people who are protected from all the bother the maintaining of a house involves: those who have staff to do it for them. I only appreciated what a difference this could make when I started researching a biography of Elizabeth Barrett Browning, who never in her life had to interrupt her writing to deal with plumbers, electricians and builders. Other upheavals in the houses she lived in certainly affected her work but not the dreary detail. Yet the state of these houses, what was being done to them even if this didn't involve her, influenced the progress of her work. Her various houses each had their own atmosphere and this atmosphere in turn affected her mood and her poetry. I'd always thought it a bit of nonsense for biographers to argue that visiting the houses their subjects had lived in was essential to understanding them but I gradually changed my mind. There is, after all, often something a house can tell you that hadn't been obvious, or hadn't been sufficiently stressed before.

That, at any rate, was my justification for going to visit every house Elizabeth Barrett Browning lived in. I knew before I went there that Coxhoe Hall, six miles south of Durham, where she was born, was a ruin, and I knew, too, that since she left it when she was a mere three years old it was of little significance. But I still wanted to see what there was to see, to begin the story of her life where it had, in fact, begun. I think maybe I'd had a vague notion that Coxhoe Hall might have been in, or near, a mining area, but it could not have been more rural. It wasn't set among blackened pits, or among bleak northern moors. It once stood on a slight rise, not far from a village, off a turning after the crossroads. The remains of the original gates were there, and the back wall of the old house, but otherwise the site was cleared. There was a good view over fields to hills beyond, with everything looking green and pleasant. The old walled garden, in which Elizabeth Barrett Browning's mother had walked when pregnant with her, was densely overgrown. Huge beech trees behind where the house had been made the place secluded, which Elizabeth's father, in particular, had liked.

So, a beginning, but not much to be gleaned there, though I was still glad I'd gone, if just because it made me feel closer to Mary, Elizabeth's mother. She never wanted to be moved from her family home in the north-east (which her husband came to share with her, when he married her, his own family home long since left in Jamaica). But she had no choice about leaving to go to Herefordshire where Edward Moulton Barrett had bought an estate of 475 acres which included farmland, woodland and parkland. Hope End was a seventeenth-century mansion, lying in a hollow, circled by low hills. Edward immediately had the Queen Anne house knocked down and an oriental-style house built, with neo-Turkish minarets, cast-iron domelets and a massive glass dome. Inside, this utterly out-of-keeping flamboyance continued, with a vast circular drawing room, decorated Italian style, mahogany doors inlaid with mother-of-pearl, crimson flock wallpaper in the dining room and brass balustrades which, Mary wrote to her mother, reminded her of the *Arabian Nights*.

But it was all demolished in 1873, so once more I couldn't enter a house where Elizabeth lived, and this time the house had been incredibly important to her development and much loved by her. She spent twenty-five years there and when the time came could hardly bear to leave it. But all was not lost, because it was the situation of Hope End that was most important to her, and that has hardly changed.

'Hope End' means 'closed valley', and that is precisely what it feels like. The house that stands there now, near to where the Barrett house stood, is hidden until the last moment, whichever direction it is approached from. There is total quiet, only the birds making any sound, all the way along from what was once the south gate of the estate. Trees of many varieties, including lots of firs, shelter the grassy paths where, in spring, the aconites Elizabeth loved still bloom. It would never have been possible, in the house, to know anyone was coming until they arrived, visitors from an outside world which barely seemed to exist. It is all quite eerie. 'I love every stone and blade of grass,' wrote the young Elizabeth, and the location of the house she spent her childhood and youth living in, still evokes the atmosphere which wrapped itself round her.

A visit, then, that helped understand her, but I still hadn't actually been inside any of the houses which influenced her. Until Wimpole Street. The very address, thanks to the play and film *The Barretts of Wimpole Street*, conjures up immediately a forbidding image. Number 50, where the family came to live after a brief and disastrous spell in Sidmouth and a short stay in Gloucester Place, was destroyed by a bomb in the Second World War. But the other houses in that long street are intact, so it was possible to go into one of them and see a room (now an office) which corresponded to Elizabeth's third-floor room at the back of the house, and look out, as she did, on the 'high star-raking chimneys'. It faced south-west, so it got the late afternoon and early evening sun, which suited her daily routine. Her room, crowded with furniture and books and busts of poets and philosophers, was very different from the almost bare office I stood in, but the same stillness she described was there. Even in twentieth-century

London, where continuous traffic thunders past, it couldn't be heard. In Hope End, the entire house had been cut off, sealed from the world; in Wimpole Street, Elizabeth's room was equally protected. The only great difference was the view.

50 Wimpole Street is often referred to as Elizabeth Barrett Browning's 'prison' from which she struggled to escape, hating the house, but it was only towards the end of her time there that she wanted to leave it. Most of the years she spent within that house, she appreciated being at the heart of London. It excited her, when the family moved there, to think of living in a house so near to famous places she'd read about, and which gave access to so many literary luminaries who would never have come anywhere near Hope End. She would never have had the chance there, of meeting them, as, in some cases, she eventually did. Wimpole Street may be a rather daunting, austere street, with its tall, terraced houses, all so grey and colourless with no greenery in sight, but it was a good address to have. It was near enough also to Regent's Park, where Elizabeth became strong enough to walk, and only a short carriage ride from Hampstead Heath, with its illusion of countryside.

But it is the next house which best emphasises the importance to Elizabeth Barrett Browning of the building she lived in, and it was not a whole house at all. Her love for it was passionate. Robert Browning took a year's lease on six unfurnished rooms in the Casa Guidi in Florence. The building they were in had once been a palace, and was opposite the side of the San Felice church which meant the windows looked out on a stone wall. There was a terrace outside the drawing room and dining room, very narrow but just broad enough for Elizabeth and her husband to walk up and down. They had space to put plant pots filled with greenery to compensate for the lack of any garden. All the rooms, except the kitchen, were huge and high-ceilinged, which made them cool, a great advantage in the summer heat of Florence.

I knew all this before I visited, and had a layout clear in my head, but the Casa Guidi still was a surprise. Coming into the building from the street it seemed so dark, as though all the light and dazzling brightness of Florence had been left behind, and that the stairs were leading into a great gloom. The entrance hall to the Brownings' apartment is narrow, with a stained-glass partition dividing it from the first room, the dining room, which was empty (at the time I saw it) and had no particular atmosphere, but then going on into the drawing room then the bedroom everything changed. Both of these rooms retain the charm they had for Elizabeth and match, uncannily, her descriptions in letters. The drawing room is twenty by thirty-three feet, the ceiling 'immensely high', and here she wrote her poetry. It was a room which that day seemed full of shadows even though there was no one in it, the brilliance of the outside sun filtering through the long windows at an angle but not reaching the corners, where anyone could lurk. The bedroom was even more mysterious, the light here subdued. It contains the bed in which Elizabeth gave birth to her only child, a son, and in which she died. It really is an emotional experience to stand there, in the half light, remembering what happened in this room, and remembering especially what the Casa Guidi meant to Elizabeth. She was never really happy away from it, always longing when, during the fierce summer heat, another house was rented in the hills, to return there, to her home which was like no other she'd ever lived in (though never one she owned). The Casa Guidi, her 'house', gave her not only deep pleasure and satisfaction but also strength. It made her feel safe and secure and lucky. She felt protected within its walls, with Robert at her side, and a new creative power surged through her poetry.

Five years later, I felt the power a house can have in the life and work of a writer even more strongly when I researched another biography, this time of Daphne du Maurier. Menabilly, the house on the Gribbin peninsula in Cornwall where she lived for twenty-five years, gave her a physical thrill when first she came across it, hidden as it was among trees and situated so that it could not be seen from the nearby sea. It was not the grand stately house, owned by the Rashleigh family, which she had imagined when she heard about it, but instead a two-storey, long, low house, the walls covered so thickly with ivy that most of the many windows were half obliterated. She thought it looked asleep, and that it had a melancholy air about it which she wanted to investigate, and which attracted her. This reaction, which sounded so fanciful, so fey, made immediate sense to me only when I saw the house. Finding it is still difficult and this difficulty seemed exciting, like being on a quest in some fairy tale. The walk from the house through the woods, to the little beach described in *Rebecca*, is intensely quiet and looking back, the house rapidly disappears, long before the sea is reached, as though it has been spirited away. This was what the secretive Daphne du Maurier had always yearned for, a house to match that part of herself which was the writer.

But though the influence of living in Menabilly was immense, it could never belong to her. She spent a quarter of a century restoring it, which cost a fortune, knowing, and dreading, that one day, when the lease was up, she would have to leave it. Reading in her letters about this passion she had for Menabilly it seemed so exaggerated to identify, to the extent she did, with a house. I'd studied drawings of it, and seen lots of photographs, but nevertheless nothing made sense until I saw it and wandered about inside, the bats swooping about in the kitchen. Then, the fascination the house had for her didn't seem so hard to understand. While she was living for a short time in Egypt, she wrote that in her dreams she was always imagining she was in Menabilly, hallucinating almost, so that when she woke up and found she was not she was sick with disappointment and a strange kind of grief. The house, without a doubt, fuelled her imagination, her love for it burning through her work.

Menabilly is a perfect example of the power a house can have.

GRASMOOR HOUSE

Loweswater
Cumbria

In the late 1980s, we began to think we could do something we'd long wanted to do, which was live and work half the year in the Lake District, from May to October. But we couldn't do it in our Caldbeck cottage, though it had served us well for a decade. It was ideal for holidays, but there was no space there for both of us to have a room to write in. And, besides, we wanted to be near a lake.

The children, in any case, weren't any longer coming with us every school holiday because two of them were by then no longer at school. Caitlin was in America, doing an MA after graduating from Sussex university, and Jake was in Italy for a year before going up to Cambridge. Only Flora still came with us, often with two of her cousins, all of them sleeping in the barn which we'd converted into a loft and a games room. But soon she, too, would be off, and we wanted to be ready.

So, a little early, we started looking for a house. It couldn't be too far away from Carlisle, because we needed to visit our parents often, and we didn't want a large house. Preferably, it would not be in a village but, on the other hand, nor would it be entirely isolated. We started off looking in the Ullswater area, but nothing suitable came up. Then, one April day in 1987, we went to look at a house in the Lorton Valley within easy reach of three lakes, Loweswater, Crummock Water and Buttermere. We drove from Caldbeck along the back roads, passing Bassenthwaite before climbing the winding road over Whinlatter Pass. The view of the valley below, when we came over the pass, showed a swooping line of fells, Grasmoor on the left, Melbreak to the right, and straight ahead, in the far distance, Red Pike and Haystacks. The route through the valley twisted and turned and finally crested on Scale Hill before dipping dizzily down to a bridge over the river Cocker. The house we were going to see was over the bridge and down a little slip road, where a sign said 'No road to the lake', though our map showed the lake,

Crummock Water, was very near, a mere few hundred yards away.

The house was on a slight rise, so that from the gate we looked up to it. This gate, painted green, was an old wooden gate, set in a tall thick hawthorn hedge. There were fir trees growing either side which had been trained to form an arch across the entry to the path up to the house. This path, going straight up, had box hedges all the way either side. The garden sloped upwards and looked attractively unkempt with daffodils bunched in thick clumps all over it. The house was double-fronted with a pretty porch in the centre. The windows were large, especially for this part of the world where windows were usually kept small to keep out the weather. It looked quite an eighteenth-century sort of house, but the estate agent's details said it was built in 1869. There were lots of houses we'd gone to see which I wouldn't even step inside, because from the first glimpse they didn't appeal to me. But this one certainly appealed.

Inside, the rooms were all empty, and had been vigorously cleaned. It looked as though it had been scrubbed from top to bottom, though all this cleaning couldn't conceal the general shabbiness and poor state of repair. But that was a plus, meaning we could start from scratch and not have to put up with ripping out perfectly good fixtures we didn't like. There were two rooms either side of the hall on the ground floor, with one of them, the kitchen, looking as if it hadn't been touched since 1869 itself. The staircase had a gracefully curved banister following the stairs round, and upstairs there was a bathroom and four bedrooms, all with these long windows looking out onto Grasmoor, and just a glint of the lake. It wasn't a sunny spring day, but the light throughout the house was strong – it was full of light.

Before we went back to Caldbeck, we walked round the area. Loweswater was a hamlet rather than a village, its centre the sixteenth-century pub, the Kirkstile, and the church, St Bartholomew's. Other cottages straggled along the road, but there were not many of them. There was no shop, and though there was a school house it had long since stopped functioning as such. The little road 'our' house was on led to a lonning (a lane) which went through fields of cows and sheep to the lake, a ten-minute walk. Once at the lake, we found another path leading to Lauthwaite Woods, making a circular tour back to the house. By the time we'd finished this preliminary exploration, we were desperate to buy the house. It was the perfect size, and in the almost perfect situation, surrounded by fells we longed to climb (and one of which we already had, on an outing from Caldbeck).

The house, called Jenkin's Hill, then, was to be auctioned at the Globe Inn in Cockermouth on 7th May. By then, we would be back in London, but we were advised it would be wise to attend the auction if we really wanted the house. Leaving a bid, or appointing someone to act for us, wouldn't allow for all kinds of imponderables. Bidding was expected to be competitive and the auction well attended. So Hunter went by train, booking in for the night at the Scale Hill Hotel. Before he left, we agreed on the maximum price we could afford, which was roughly based on what we thought we'd get for the Caldbeck cottage plus the Algarve house. The auctioneer alarmed Hunter by saying, in his introductory remarks, that this house was in 'the loveliest of valleys' where houses rarely came up for sale. The bids came in thick and fast, which was apparently unusual at Cumbrian auctions, and rapidly reached then passed our agreed limit. Hunter and one other bidder, not there in person, hung on in there, inching upwards more slowly, until the stand-in for the other bidder had reached his instructed limit, and withdrew, and the house became ours.

There was an excitement about buying this house. It was going to be as important to our lives, we felt, as Boscastle Road had been. As Virginia Woolf put it, when she and her husband bought Monk's House, it would be 'as though one clapped on a solid half-globe to one's London life'. And there was the excitement of a new area which offered delights Caldbeck couldn't deliver, such as the prospect of swimming in the lake and climbing all the surrounding high fells. Our cottage had been in a wild, bare landscape which had its own appeal but now we would be in an almost lush landscape by comparison, full of trees, thickly green and verdant. Once we'd had the renovations carried out we would also be living in what amounted to luxury so far as space went – after the cramped nature of the cottage – with a room each to write in.

We sold the Caldbeck cottage in October 1987, and moved into what we renamed Grasmoor House that same half-term week (Flora was still at school). Renaming the house was not, we realised, a wise or popular thing to do. We knew local people would frown upon it, thinking it a bit of a cheek when the name Jenkin's Hill actually appeared on some maps. But the renaming was for a good reason. The nearest house to it was named 'Jenkin', and there was endless confusion possible over which was 'Jenkin' and which 'Jenkin's Hill'. We renamed ours Grasmoor House, after the fell it faced. It made the house seem instantly more 'ours', as though no one had lived there before us.

But they had, and the signs were everywhere. The master carpenter had crafted exquisite floors of pine. The boards were broad and closely fitted and needed only a coat of seal to reveal the deep golden colour. There were shutters on the ground floor rooms, equally well made, and when we pulled apart modern electric fires it was to reveal old fireplaces with tiled backs to them, each tile a Victorian artwork. It seemed marvellously ironic that as a girl I'd hated our old-fashioned, black leaded range and here I was thrilled to find we had in our house fireplaces I would be happy to black-lead myself. We tested the fires and they worked perfectly, except for one in our bedroom which had been blocked up. We'd be able to have log fires. It was no good mocking ourselves – 'real log fires' were the thing for the country idyll.

The builder we hired to do all the changes we wanted was no J.P. Brown and he didn't employ unskilled labourers. The carpenter who worked for him was a perfectionist who used the best materials and wouldn't tolerate a single ill-fitting joint. He was slow, and we were impatient, but he wouldn't be hurried. When we urged him to take some short cut to get the kitchen ready sooner, he just gave us a look, and said nothing, and continued at the same rate. Sometimes we changed our minds about how we wanted something done when he was already halfway through doing it, and neither of us dared to tell him. We hinted at a possible change, and he looked appalled, so we hurriedly said it didn't really matter, that of course we wouldn't want him to rip out the immaculate work he'd already done.

It was six months before the house was as we wanted it and we were ready to begin living and working there half the year (though, in fact, it was another two years before we began doing that, the full May–October, when Flora was eighteen). The woman who had lived

there before us had run it as a bed and breakfast estab-
lishment as well as a tea-place. Her teas had been famous
for her cakes and tarts and scones, all of which she'd
produced out of what seemed to me a Stone-Age kitchen.
She was still living locally when we moved in and I thought
she might like to see what we'd done (or rather had had
done) to the house, so I invited her to tea. I worried that
she might find it a little upsetting, visiting the house which
had been her home for something like twenty years, and
where her husband had recently died, but she was on the
contrary curious and eager to see the alterations. She loved
the room we'd made into a kitchen, exclaiming over the
pine cupboards more than over the new cooker and hob,
and was astonished to see the huge L-shaped bedroom
made out of two of the old bedrooms. The bathroom was
completely revamped, but she was pleased we kept the
large old-fashioned tub which she said had been nearly
new and it would've grieved her to see it thrown out. Then
we had tea. I'd made a cake and offered a piece to her in
that self-deprecating middle-class manner I'd picked up.
'Have a piece of this cake,' I said, 'though I'm sure it won't
be as delicious as the cakes, I hear, you made.' She took
a piece, ate half of it, thought for a moment, and then

said, being a Cumbrian, 'No, it isn't, but thank you, it's very nice.'

So began, in 1990, the living of two lives, our London life, in Boscastle Road, and our country life, in Grasmoor House, Loweswater. It wasn't at all like having a holiday house in the Algarve, or Northamptonshire, or a bolt-hole in Caldbeck. The switch – either way but especially from London to Loweswater – was, and is, always fraught, the build-up to the going looming large with so much to be remembered and organised. There was always someone moving into Boscastle Road to look after it, with the deal that it would be rent- and bill-free in return for the garden being kept tidy and the house safe and clean. Usually, these house-sitters were friends of our children who needed temporary accommodation and had no money to rent anywhere, or sometimes it was friends between flats 'who had a gap to fill'. My theory was that if I left the house in near perfect order then it would be in the same condition when I returned, so setting my standards high took exhausting effort. Going the other way was much easier. Grasmoor House was smaller and it had mostly just been the two of us living there so there was less to do. Also, from the beginning I'd been determined to keep it as simple and uncluttered as possible, not heaped with possessions of one sort or another, as Boscastle Road was after nearly thirty years of five of us living in it.

Arriving at Grasmoor House what impressed me, always, was the atmosphere of calm. It's a quiet house, looking outwards towards the high fells all around and somehow absorbing their unchanging nature. The silence inside is intense, as though the walls are noise proofed throughout, and this makes moving around it an unhurried affair. We don't thunder around, running up and down stairs, or banging doors violently as we are inclined to do in London, always rushing, but instead take our time. On the surface, my life continues exactly as it does in Boscastle Road – write in the mornings, walk in the afternoons, read in the evenings – but it feels quite different. The difference is due to the situation of the respective houses. In Grasmoor House, there are no interruptions, and nothing is happening all around. I look out on the flank of Melbreak and the rising spur of Hen Comb and know nothing has changed in hundreds of years. There is nothing man-made to disturb the undulating line of the horizon. Sometimes there are sheep on the fell sides, sometimes not, and that is the extent of the variety. There is no sound of traffic, only of the wind in the giant ash tree, or the strangled cry of a sheep caught in a hedge. If the telephone rings, it is thunderously loud.

Unlike our cottage in Caldbeck, this house has no lingering feeling of hard lives once lived here even if they were. It seems made for a certain standard of living, one in which separate rooms were allocated to sleep in, eat in, relax in, and study in. It was never a cottage and it was not a farm house, which gave it a pointed status compared to other buildings in the village. When we bought it, it didn't look very attractive, because the walls were a dirty grey stucco and the windows had a border painted round them, Lake District style, which was a dark, dreary green, but once the exterior was painted off-white and the surrounds on the windows white, it looked fresher and more gracious, coming into its own. Wordsworth, of course, would not have approved, believing, as he did, that buildings should blend into the landscape and not stand out from it. He didn't like seeing these white dots scattered over the countryside, especially if they were on hillsides, but we loved having our house as a point of reference when we looked down upon it from the top of Grasmoor or Melbreak.

Sometimes, walking along old bridle paths, we would come across the ruins of a house, tucked away in the folds of a fell side, far from any road. It's hard to imagine how such houses were ever built in these inaccessible situations. How was all the material needed brought to it, the cement, the wood, the pipes? The stones are nearby, the same sort of stones the dry stone walls are built of, but everything else would have to be ferried over rough ground for a mile at least, probably in a cart. Someone wanted to build their house in these locations badly enough to go through organising all this laborious business, and now it was a ruin, abandoned long ago. Such a disturbing sight, these ruins. So much of the basic structure remains, the clear outline of how the rooms were arranged, even though the roof has gone and all the doors and windows. Stepping over the collapsed front wall and peering into corners there is always the carcass of a bird lying there and often the detritus of some fell walkers' picnic. The wind and rain will have stripped the interior of plaster and paint, but the floors will still have the remains of coverings, odd patches of broken tiles showing

235

through the dirt, a reminder that the place was once lived in. The local people will know the story of any ruined house. They will have tales of who built it and why, and of what happened when it was vacated and left to rot, instead of being sold and passed on to someone else. But the ruined house tells its own tale of some mistake, some disaster that could not be surmounted. Better, I always think, that it should be levelled, every stone removed, because what remains is not just sad but frightening – a house, a solid stone house, reduced to this.

We walked, we climbed, and we swam. The lake was where we spent our afternoons whenever there was hot weather, taking a picnic down to the tiny pebble beach known as Sandy Yat. 'Yat' means 'gate', and a gate is still there, but if there was ever sand it has long since been washed away. The view from Sandy Yat is of the whole of Crummock Water stretching away to Buttermere, an expanse of water which, on still days, is literally like a mirror, reflecting perfectly the fells all around. Going into it to swim, the aim was not to shatter these reflections, to swim so carefully that in spite of a slight ripple on the surface they were undisturbed. It was as if we were moving not through water but through hills. Once, on such a day,

I got up before dawn and slipped out of the house – I felt it held its breath for me – and walked rapidly along the side of Melbreak to Buttermere so that by the time the sun was up I was climbing Red Pike and stood on the summit by nine o'clock with the sun bouncing off the lake below in a million tiny lights as it hit the water. There was the sensation, standing alone there, of being completely insubstantial, of having no place amid all this natural glory, of disappearing into the landscape. I thought how satisfying it would be, when the time came to die, to die in such a place, just melting into the rocks. It wasn't a morbid thought at all, but quite the opposite. Then I came down and swam from Ling Crag.

This was our alternative life, but we always knew that however much we loved it our real home was in Boscastle Road and if we had to choose there would be no contest. The missing elements, wonderful though our Loweswater summers proved to be, were largely human ones. In London were our children and, eventually, grand-children, and our friends, friends of many years, and work connections (for Hunter especially). And, as the nights drew in come October, there were theatres and cinemas and art galleries, and all the cultural riches London offers. There was also a kind of trigger London pulls which starts ideas off whereas, for us, the Lake District soothed rather than fired us. Great for working when ideas had taken root but not, in our case, so great for thinking of them. We returned each October refreshed and refuelled though within days we'd be shattered already, barely able to cope with ordinary things like crossing a busy road. We had, each autumn, to learn again the art of city living – but it was always exciting, exhilarating. We might feel faithless to Grasmoor House, but we were home.

THE HOUSE NOW

2013

The older I became, the more I liked being in my house. When I did go out, coming home to it was always a relief, however shabby it was becoming. By the year 2000, when we'd been in it nearly forty years, I could see that it needed redecorating. Curtains were well worn and faded, and sofas sagging with children endlessly jumping on them. But it was familiar and relaxing, and I couldn't bring myself to care about that horrible word 'refurbishing'.

I was by then becoming a less than good housewife. Virginia Woolf once wrote to a friend, 'Does housekeeping interest you at all? I think it ought to be just as good as writing, and I never see . . . where the separation between the two comes in . . . my theory is that they mix indistinguishably.' An odd thing to say, especially as Virginia Woolf would never be thought of as any kind of housewife, amazed as she once was to discover what an effort it took her to wash the dishes after dinner. But I'd found that being a housewife as well as a writer could be made to work perfectly well, without any help, so long as the energy and the ability to organise time were still there.

I used to like saying, when anyone asked me what I did, that I was a housewife. If I wasn't actually in the process of writing something that was what I reckoned I was, even though the very word 'housewife' is now denigrated. Nobody calls herself a housewife, for goodness' sake. It's taken to mean a woman who 'just' looks after a house and does nothing else. What can one say to such a poor creature? Best say nothing, and smile, and turn pityingly aside. How, after all, can a woman marry a house? It's ridiculous. Unless it's said – 'I'm a housewife' – with a self-deprecating laugh, making it clear this is a joke, it embarrasses people. If it's said for real, humbly, the listener will be horrified and hope you will crawl away quickly before their expression reveals contempt.

How this came about I'm not sure, but it happened after the end of the Second World War. Until then, for a

woman to say she was a housewife was perfectly acceptable.
Then, within twenty years, it became something of a term
of abuse, especially when the word 'little' was put in front
of it – 'Oh, she's just a little housewife', meaning one-of-
little-brain. Mrs Thatcher made things worse by proclaiming
her own 'housewife' qualities. It is partly the word itself
that does the harm, conjuring up a ludicrous image. A
'housekeeper' sounds better but carries with it servant
status; a 'house manager' would be better still, since it
could mean man or woman, and a proper job; or maybe
the term that emerged in the seventies is best of all as an
alternative to the unfortunate 'housewife': doesn't 'I'm a
home economist' sound grand?

But still, no one wants to define herself as one
whose role in life is to look after the running of a house.
It's strange, because it is an exacting job requiring all kinds
of skills, the sort most people don't even notice never mind
value. Any woman in charge of the running of a house
fights a constant battle against the ever rising tide of disorder
and dirt, and even if she can happily, and sensibly, settle
for a certain degree of mess, there is still all the provisioning
and the laundry and the cooking to be done – I'd say a
housewife doing all this on her own and doing it well is

something of a heroine. Or a fool. Either way, the pressure is relentless, in spite of all the brilliant labour-saving devices in modern life, with the house demanding constant attention. If it doesn't get it, it shows its disapproval pretty quickly and becomes a place no longer a pleasure to live in.

So I let things slide a bit as I grew older, with the influences of housewives in my northern family fading over the years. My standards became those of my neighbourhood, which on the whole, with a few startling exceptions, were fairly lax. Walking round our streets in the evening, and peering through windows into rooms with lights blazing but curtains/blinds/shutters as yet undrawn, a favourite ploy of writers, I saw a good deal of 'relaxed living' on display. It looked attractive. Families sitting round big messy tables, children coming and going, taking what they wanted from the dishes of food, the telly on in the corner, a dog wandering around, books and newspapers in heaps, sofas with torn covers – all must be well in such a house regardless of who is looking after it. A fallacy, probably, but not one that's going to be exposed by looking through a window.

Often, going out to post a letter at dusk, I've left the shutters open in our living room so that on my way back I can walk on the other side of the road and peer in, as though I didn't live there at all. The room I see bears all the distinguishing marks of those other rooms I've looked into except that it is at the moment empty of people, and tidy. There are the usual shelves of books, the paintings on the walls, the general impression of a comfortable space. Our lights don't fit in, though. Our lamps are old, table lamps, with apricot-coloured shades, which look pretty but are hopeless for reading under, though such a lot of reading goes on. We moan about our lighting every winter, and swear we will have fitted those small, strong bulbs that other people have shining brightly from their ceilings, but we never do, unable to face the upheaval involved. Still, standing and staring into our living room, the glow from these useless lamps is soft and pleasant. They give the room a comfortable look, maybe very retro but worn, relaxed, a mature room. There are so many things that should be done to it, but it pleases me. My house, for all its deficiencies, pleases me.

This is lucky, because I've no energy now to change anything about it. The relief that I used to feel coming back into our house during the time, in the late 1970s, when cancer began is even more intense now that, since 2007, it is metastatic, spreading through my bones and into the lining of the right lung. Inside my house, I can cope. I resist leaving it for anything more than a walk on the Heath, for as far as I can manage. Yet I don't feel confined the rest of the time, I don't feel like screaming at the sight of the walls. When everything in my body is changing, as the cancer advances, my house, by staying the same, is a huge comfort, as it always has been.

For a while, during several months in 2007, it took on a new role, one room within it becoming like a small hospital ward. It wasn't a room exactly suited to the purpose, but it was on the ground floor at the back, the room made out of the old coalhouse, kitchen and yard. It has a large window and glass doors leading into the garden. The table was removed and the chairs round it, and a single bed placed across it so that lying down I looked out onto the garden. Beside this bed, I had a Zimmer frame, and with its help could just about get myself to the lavatory and washroom off the hall. I never entirely lost the use of my legs but I'd come dangerously close to it, and whether I'd get back to being able to walk properly again wasn't known. I might, I might not. Meanwhile, I'd better adapt to life in one room.

I did, remarkably quickly. After all, I was home,

in my house, with its famous (for me) healing properties, after weeks in the Royal Free, since the cancer erupted again. The extraordinary thing to me was how slow I'd been to realise what was happening, considering I always knew it might, and never for one moment considered myself 'cured', in spite of the passage of almost thirty years. I missed the significance of the first signs, which would've been spotted if I'd gone on having annual check-ups at the Royal Marsden, but these had been discontinued by them, after ten years, when Mr McKinna retired. The difficulty, as for all people with a history of cancer, is that not every twinge, or similar, is a warning sign, especially as one ages, and arthritis, and muscular strains, cause pain. So when, swimming in the Caribbean in January 2007, I felt a twinge of pain between my shoulder blades, I put it down to exactly that, a muscular strain. I also saw that I had what looked like an insect bite on one of the old mastectomy scars, but then I had them on my legs too. We came home at the beginning of February and though I wasn't swimming all day long any more, the twinge of pain between my shoulder blades was still there with every movement and the insect bite on the scar hadn't gone, though those on my legs had. I didn't even think about going to my GP, and not out of any fear that these minor things might be significant. I was sixty-nine, it was wear-and-tear, and otherwise I was in splendid health.

Then something odd started happening to my walk. I was a fast walker, tending to stride, and suddenly this rapid striding felt lopsided. Instead of following the path up Parliament Hill, I was veering onto the grass and having constantly to correct my direction. So, at last, I went to my GP. I saw a young doctor I'd never seen before, but then I hadn't been to the practice for years. This doctor listened to my rather apologetic account of why I'd come and examined me carefully. I pointed out the insect bite, though it hardly needed to be pointed out, suggesting that really it was nothing. It was concluded that what I was suffering from was indeed muscular strain, and the insect bite was just a spot in a delicate place. I was told to come back in ten days' time if the walking hadn't righted itself. I left the surgery cheerful, and went off to review a book for the BBC Radio 4 *Front Row* programme. Unfortunately, getting off the bus, my cheerfulness evaporated. I could hardly walk the few yards into Broadcasting House.

But to cut this sad tale short, before those ten days were up I was in the Royal Free, an emergency admission, with what turned out to be multiple metastatic lesions and a vertebral collapse, causing spinal cord compression. The insect bite/spot was another lesion. By the time I was admitted, I was numb from the chest downwards, but I still had bladder and bowel control, and minimal use of my legs. There was a long wait until the Royal Marsden, to which a biopsy of the tumour had been sent, confirmed that these lesions were a spread from the one I'd been treated for in 1978. I was told that I now had secondary breast cancer, for which there is no cure, though it could be controlled.

Controlled: I rolled the word round and round in my head. What does, in this context, 'controlled' mean? What is the difference between 'control' and 'cure'? A substantial one, I thought. If something is cured, it has gone. It is finished, over. But if it is controlled, it is always present, if held back. Who, or what, does this controlling? Drugs helped by radiotherapy and, some-times, surgery. Drugs, in my case hormonal therapies, a whole range of them, were to do this controlling, acting as a brake. Immediately, I imagined that I was on a bicycle, going very fast down one of the Lake District mountain passes, and I was braking hard to negotiate tricky bends. It was quite a comforting image. But then I remembered that brakes often fail when under such pressure and that brake linings wear out. How would I know when they reached this stage? Could new brake linings be put in? Not without the bike stopping, idiot.

So that was how I came to be confined to bed in my house. It seemed such a triumph to be there at all, the relief and pleasure making me light-headed (though maybe the drugs, and the radiotherapy, and the lack of sleep in the oncology ward, had done that anyway). For ages, days and days, I was content to lie there, repeating in my head, over and over again: 'home, home, home'. I was safe again in my house. It was like being in a nest, and at first this didn't seem at all limiting. I had no energy, so I didn't want to leave this safe and secure place where everything was arranged according to my needs. I could, and did, lie for hours looking out onto the garden, at its springtime best, the cherry and apple and pear trees all in bud and about to blossom. I'd fix my attention on one particular cluster of buds on one particular branch and convince myself I could witness them opening second by second. The weather, towards the end of March, was warm and sunny, and usually I would have been out on the Heath all afternoon, but I seemed not to mind being in the house. I didn't read and I didn't write. I just looked. At the garden, at paintings, at photographs.

But, of course, this could not go on. Every day I lolled in bed, what remained of my muscles was being eroded. If I didn't want to stay for ever as an invalid I had to exercise, so I began following the instructions the physiotherapist in the Royal Free had given me. Then, as I became a little stronger, an occupational therapist came to show me how to use crutches so that I could progress from the Zimmer frame. Patiently, she demonstrated, one foot forward, one crutch forward – simple. But no, it wasn't. I put the wrong leg with the wrong crutch, and stood immobile in the middle of the room. It was pathetic, and being pathetic was something I could not bear. So, fury with myself made me try harder and eventually (useful word, when I can't actually remember how long it took) I mastered crutches. The next stage was to leave the house to go for regular physiotherapy sessions at the Marie Curie Hospice in Hampstead.

This was a big step. I didn't want to leave the house, not for anything. If I was going to force myself to do it, I wanted all the curtains and blinds of the houses in our road to be drawn, the way they used to be for a funeral when I was growing up in Carlisle. I didn't want anyone to see me staggering to the car on my crutches. I wanted to close my own eyes – dangerous – so that if anyone was walking past I wouldn't see them and wouldn't have to talk to them. I made such a meal of it, getting from the house to the car, that I was exhausted with the tension. Looking out of the car window, it seemed incredible that people were walking without thinking about it, walking at a great pace along the pavements, oblivious to what a miracle this is once you can't do it.

Going into the hospice was difficult. I'd been there before, to visit my sister-in-law who had respite care there before she died, so the building itself was familiar and not at all alarming, just a large, Edwardian mansion converted for this other purpose. But being a visitor and being a patient are different experiences. I tried to get to the gym without looking into any other room and without talking to anyone. I would have liked blinkers on, really. In the background, I could hear pleasant, reassuring noises, people laughing and chatting, but I didn't want to respond to any of it. I wanted to do what I'd come to do then get back to my house as soon as possible. A lamentable attitude, but it was mine.

I spent an hour there, three times a week, for two months, working on the machines, watched over by a charming young French physiotherapist. Naturally, I couldn't keep up my attitude of not wanting to have anything to do with anyone else. So many people were in a much worse state than I was and had been brought in wheelchairs to do simple arm exercises. Most were returning home after their sessions, but there was one woman who doubted she would be able to go home because she lived in a flat on the second floor and needed a stairlift which was proving awkward to fit, so she was going to have to stay in the hospice while it was 'sorted'. I imagined not being able to go back to my house . . . too awful to go on contemplating. I only ever managed to enter the hospice because I knew that within an hour I'd be leaving it to go home and yet I knew that one day it was very likely I would be staying there. Gloom.

It took six weeks for me to graduate to being a one-crutch user, and then, after another four, I took two unaided steps – the excitement definitely worth an exclamation mark! 'Don't try this at home yet,' the physiotherapist warned me, pointing out that I'd had a rail either side of me, to grab onto if needed when I 'walked', and that she herself had been standing close by. But as soon as I got home, I went into the garden and, with Hunter on one side and the children on the other and behind me, ready to catch me, I walked. Six steps. No collapse. After that, the crutches were replaced with a walking stick, though not the one provided by the Royal Free. I used a stick that had been my father's, and before that his father's, an old-fashioned gnarled stick made of ash. My legs felt as if they were encased in plaster, they were so awkward and heavy, but I could totter short distances even if I was not yet up to the Heath.

This stubborn reluctance to leave the house still went on though I was now able to do it. Within it, I was regaining mobility all the time, finding myself delighted to be in rooms I hadn't managed to enter for months. I conquered the stairs and was back in our bedroom, so the 'ward' downstairs was dismantled and everything put back to normal. Lastly, by July, I made it up another flight of stairs to the room where I write, up at the top of the house. There I sat, once more at my desk, pen in hand, ready to write again. Only I didn't. I sat and sat, and stared out over the trees. For years I'd been trained the way mothers of small children are, not to waste a moment of child-free time, and so I'd always got straight down to it, and the habit had carried on even after there was no real need to be so concentrated. But now, I was tired. I couldn't do it, couldn't produce the ten A4 pages in a morning which I'd been used to. I tried to persuade myself that, through being so slow now, every word would mean more, be more tellingly crafted. Not true. My old, rapid, if careless, style of writing was better by far than the halting, lame stuff I was turning out, crawling hesitantly over one mere page in three hours. Why bother doing it? Why expend precious energy, of which there was so little, on writing, when it would be better conserved for other things? Yet each morning the lure of the desk and the pen drew me up to that room, and I gave into it. Sometimes, sitting was painful, which made sticking to the writing ridiculous. It wasn't even as though I thought I was turning out anything special enough to justify this regime – it was simply that for some strange reason I wanted to be there, doing it.

At the time, I was working on a novel, *The Unknown Bridesmaid*, and was 140 pages into it. When I went back to it, after the gap of three months while I was recovering, I couldn't remember a thing about it, and had to read the whole thing to find out who this bridesmaid was and why she was unknown. It was written in two 'voices' and I couldn't understand either of them, or where this tale was trying to go, so I had no option but to tear it up and start again. There was only a tiny seed of the original idea left and this time I had to nurture it delicately, knowing I could only write in short stretches and mustn't let the narrative get too complicated or it would swamp my feeble energy. But at least I could write, if differently and with a new caution. It pleased me to be doing it, it meant something, whatever the end result, and that was all that mattered. I didn't even care if it turned out hopeless and didn't get published – it was all about the process of the doing of it.

That year, 2007, we managed only seven weeks in Loweswater, with the need to come back for scans to determine how the drugs were controlling the cancer. It was lovely to be there at all, but the meaning of being in Grasmoor House had changed. The point of having the house had been to be able to go for long walks and climbs among the fells and without being able to do this there was a new sense of frustration. The house didn't reassure me the way Boscastle Road did – it was a house, this one, to be *out* of, however attractive inside. Then in 2008 and 2009, though stronger and now able to walk, with a stick, of course, surprisingly far, I had to keep coming back for a couple of nights to have regular scans while I was on a Cancer Research trial and this coming and going made me unsettled, never quite belonging to the country or the city. I came back by train, and I'd sit there as it approached London, all those dreary rows and rows of the backs of houses flashing past, thinking it wasn't possible that somewhere out there, in all this mess, there was one house which had a personal identity for me. It seemed absurd, unbelievable, to invest such affection in one pile of bricks and mortar to the extent that I did. It seemed a miracle that the key I had in my bag would turn the lock of the front door of one particular house. But travelling the other way, to Loweswater via Penrith, was different. The last stretch of the journey in the train saw no houses to look out on, only hills and trees, with an occasional farmhouse in the distance. The landscape dominated, imposing a great peace on everything. The small town of Penrith hardly interrupts this impression, and then I was in the car and after the drive over the Whinlatter Pass dropped down into Lorton Valley where for a long time there are no houses at all and even when they begin to appear they are all highly individual. Instead of feeling depressed, as I did at the sight of my house in London, lost among thousands of others, I'd feel cheered that in Loweswater my house could never be buried among others. It stands out, by itself, not part of any street or road or square.

All very comforting, yet I didn't adapt as well to my new circumstances in Grasmoor House. There was always the worry that if disaster struck again, which at some point it would, I'd be an uncomfortably long way from the Royal Free and the doctors who treated me. In Boscastle Road, I was ten minutes away from help; in Grasmoor House, an hour away from any hospital likely to be able to help. Being in the depths of the country is not a good place to be with my sort of disease. Going north in May, instead of being exciting, something eagerly looked forward to, now made me a little nervous. Usually, I had a CT scan before we left, and even if that showed the cancer was stable, I'd still feel apprehensive. It took me weeks to settle down and really relish the longer walks I could now do and, because of these, the longer spells of writing. It was remarkable to find that walking must be somehow related to writing, that it somehow fuelled it. I'd always enjoyed walks, and seen them as an essential part of each day, but I hadn't appreciated this strange connection. The walking loosened the writing.

I was on the lookout, of course, after the events of spring 2007, when my walking became unsteady, for any of the same signs, but the signs of danger this time had nothing to do with walking and so yet again I failed to recognise their significance. All that happened was that I had waves of pins-and-needles in my right arm. They were strong, but of short duration, and I concluded that I'd been writing too long or else carrying something that was too heavy. This was in July 2010, when we were in the Lake District, with the next appointment at the Royal Free at the end of August. The pins-and-needles came and went but otherwise I was fine, except I didn't know I wasn't. The pain itself, in my spine, didn't start until the beginning of August, and when it did it was only there when I was standing or sitting, so I thought it was my old slipped disc trouble. I ended up back in London having radiotherapy to two parts of my spine. The poor *Unknown Bridesmaid* looked like remaining unknown for ever.

It is now 2013 and I am on the last of the hormone treatments, given by injection into the muscles of the buttocks every four weeks. This is the sixth year since secondary cancer was discovered, so I am lucky not only to be still alive but to be doing remarkably well, which is to say that though I tire frighteningly easily, I can still carry on with my normal life to a surprising extent. I walk, wherever I am, for at least an hour a day, sometimes two hours (with lots of rests) and though I need a stick I am not leaning on it all the time. It's partly sheer determination that keeps me walking but determination wouldn't in itself be enough – it's much more the effect of the controlling drugs.

Soon, the control will start to slip. The hormone drugs will fail, and then it will be some sort of chemotherapy, if I agree to it. That sounds very grand – 'if I agree to it' indeed – but though I like to think I might not, I've seen how people, who have thought the same, jump at any chance, so I'm not confident that I'd say no thanks, I'm seventy-five, I'll just go. The going is the problem. Where am I to do it, this dying? The desire to die at home, in one's own bed, seems so strong in some people, as though to succumb anywhere else is a failure. Relatives speak with pride that 'he/she died at home', with their help. Since my house means to me what I've tried to show it does, you'd think I, too, will want to stay in it, to die at home, but I'm not sure that I do. I don't want to somehow taint the house by dying in it. I don't want it to become, for the period of this dying, a mini-hospice, filled with all the equipment I've seen needed: the special mattress, the device delivering morphine, maybe another for oxygen. I don't want it having all the essential, wonderful nurses trooping in and out, the district nurses, the Macmillan nurses, the Marie Curie nurses . . . I've seen it all, I know how the house would change its character, how all this would make it a place I no longer knew, its privacy shattered.

So, why not avoid this by going into a hospice? What would there be to lose if my house would no longer be itself? Well, there are other people to consider: my family. For them, it might be a lot easier to have me at home so that they wouldn't have to go backwards and forwards to a hospice. But, on the other hand, I've noticed that when people are dying in a hospice it helps distance their family and partners from the dying. The dying person, once in a hospice, is removed from their usual surroundings and this can help to prepare for the final removal. The hospice setting provides a separation which may seem hard at the time but maybe it helps. Dying at home, no matter how caring those attached to the dying person are, places a huge strain on them. Maybe I could do most of the dying at home then go into a hospice for the last bit. 'Bit?' Whatever do I mean? I make it sound as if this is some sort of game. Probably, I won't be able to make the decision anyway. It will make itself, 'events' will dictate the pace, or it will all happen more suddenly than I dare to hope.

I wouldn't, though, like to be leaving my house knowing I was never coming back to it – God, how awful that would be. I thought, this year, coming back to it after a brilliant summer, a whole four months without having to rush back to London, how much it meant to me. Suppose, while we were in the Lake District, it had been destroyed, in a fire maybe, and there was no house to come back to. What would be lost, apart from the contents? What could not be recreated by moving into some similar other house and replacing these contents? Is it the furniture/ pictures/belongings which matter? Or is this love of a house a matter of what has taken place within its walls over fifty years and has nothing to do with the building itself or the things filling it? But this history, these memories, already have a safe place in my mind. The house might disappear, but what it has represented cannot. The building, the bricks and mortar, are not important, surely.

Yet somehow the house itself, its very fabric, is of importance. An intimate knowledge of its layout, of how all the rooms are arranged and used, stimulates a weird pleasure. I *know* this house. It has been changed by us not only in the real, practical sense of altering its appearance and internal geography, but by our living within it. Instinct guides me everywhere. I don't have to wonder where I am going or what I will find. The house doesn't need to remind me of what has taken place, why certain rooms are of a significance nobody else could possibly guess. Take the building away and it is alarming to realise memories might not be enough. Something indefinable would be lost. I need the house's influence – the 'influence' that Leonard Woolf thought 'might well be the subject of a scientific investigation.'

My investigation has not been scientific, nor has it really any claims to have been an investigation, but I share Leonard Woolf's conviction that it is not 'nonsense' (as he feared) to think that a house lived in for a long time by the same people reflects something of them and gives them something back. Of Monk's House, where he and his wife Virginia lived from 1919–1941, he said it was 'the most powerful moulder' of how they lived their lives. I don't think I would go that far. Our house has not exactly 'moulded' me. But, on the other hand, it has provided a structure and a privacy which have been of immeasurable value. I was not mistaken, as a child, to believe that having a house, never mind a room, of my own was, for me, hugely important.

Coming home this year, 2013, was different from returning in other years. For the first time, we had had no one living in the house, though one or other of our children had been in and out every day. This meant that everything was as I'd left it, with no need for me to rush around arranging things how I liked them. It was as though I'd merely been out for an hour, walking on the Heath, and here I was, home again. But as I went through the various rooms and began to unpack, I thought, no, it isn't as if I've just been gone an hour. Something is different. The house knows I've been away four months. It needs to get used to me again. There's a stillness, a sense of caution in the air. The house needs to settle around me again. I'm not fully accepted yet. It takes two days to feel that finally we fit – the house and me.

And I've come full circle: as a child, I always wanted to be in other people's houses. Now, though still fascinated by those other houses, I am only really comfortable and relaxed in my own. My house is like a garment, made to my exact measurements, draped around me in the way I like. I never want to change it.